Red Hat Linux

The Official Red Hat Linux Users Guide

The Red Hat Development Team:

Donald Barnes

Kit Cosper

Marc Ewing

Erik Troan

Computer Science

Red Hat Software, Inc.
25 Sylvan Road South
Westport, CT 06880

ISBN: 1-888172-59-2

Revision 3.0, February 1996.

Red Hat Software, Inc.
25 Sylvan Road South
Westport, CT 06880
1-203-454-5500
redhat@redhat.com

Contents

Preface – What is Red Hat Linux?

Red Hat Linux is a complete operating system based on the Linux kernel. On most systems, it is easy to install: the installation script can walk you through the process in as little as 15 minutes. The installation system is very flexible: you can install and uninstall individual software "packages" with a couple of clicks of your mouse button. It is easy to maintain: package installations can be verified and corrected. It is easy to administer: a set of graphical administration tools bundled into a "control-panel" reduce the hassle of every day system administration. Complete source code is provided for everything in the system.

If you are itching to install Red Hat Linux right away, check out the Quick Start chapter. After reading that you should be able to do a basic installation without much trouble. For new Linux users, we would suggest reading through the entire manual first to get a good understanding of the various systems and installation procedures. If you have any problems installing or using Red Hat Linux please see the Frequently Asked Questions chapter **??**

We would like to thank all our beta testers for entrusting their systems to early versions of RH Linux and for taking the time to submit bug reports from the front, especially those who have been with Red Hat since the "Halloween" release, and earlier. We would also like to thank Linus Torvalds and the hundreds of developers around the world for creating, truly, one of the wonders of distributed development.

Thanks again, and welcome to the wonderful world of Linux!

Donnie Barnes, Kit Cosper, Marc Ewing, Erik Troan

Chapter 1

Red Hat History

Marc Ewing was attempting to build a software product using a Linux system as his development platform. A graduate of Carnegie Mellon and subsequently with IBM, Marc soon realized that he was spending more time managing his Linux system than he was building his product and what the world really needed was a better Linux distribution.

Linux, like Unix itself, is a very modular operating system. The skills required to select, compile, link, and install, the various components that are needed for a complete Linux OS are beyond the experience of most people who might want to use Linux. The various Linux distributions go a long way towards solving this for the average Linux user, but most do not address the problem of how to upgrade your Linux system once you get it successfully installed. Most users found it easier to delete their whole Linux system and reinstall from scratch when they needed to upgrade.

The Red Hat distribution makes Linux easier to install and maintain by providing the user with advanced package management, graphical (point and click!) system installation and control, and system administration tools.

Red Hat's first release in the fall of '94 was received to wide critical acclaim from users such as the Harvard/Smithsonian Observatory, and commercial software developers such as Caldera Inc. As the demand for Red Hat Linux grew, Red Hat Software was forced to expand with the demand. Red Hat Software first hired Donnie Barnes, a Computer Engineering graduate, and then Erik Troan, a Computer Science and Computer Engineering graduate, both out of North Carolina State University. Kit Cosper, a Computer Science graduate of UNC Wilmington is the newest member of the Red Hat team.

With its second release in May '95, Red Hat gained wide acceptance on the Internet and by most of the major Linux internet archive distributors such as Pacific Hi-Tech, InfoMagic, and Yggdrasil. In a short time, Red Hat Linux has become widely accepted and has many users. We look forward to serving even more customers in the future!

Chapter 2

Free Software

2.1 The Free Software Model

Probably the best feature of Linux is that it is distributable under the terms of the GNU Public License (GPL). This feature has allowed research institutions, universities, commercial enterprises, and hackers, to develop and use Linux and related technologies co-operatively without fear that their work would someday be controlled and restricted by a commercial vendor.

In short, the GPL changes the model of software development and distribution to one much like the model our Legal system and its industry uses. If a lawyer designs an argument that wins his case in front of the supreme court his reward is not only the fees his client pays him but also the additional clients that his achievement attracts to his practice. The "argument" he used becomes available for any other lawyer to use without restriction, and in fact becomes part of our collective legal heritage.

This new model is already a new industry with companies like Cygnus Support (see `http://www.cygnus.com`) becoming multi-million dollar enterprises on the basis of providing support and services for large commercial users of GPL'd and other "freely distributable" software. Red Hat Software, Inc.'s rapid growth is based, similarly, on our development and support of the Red Hat Linux distribution, a product that we distribute worldwide on CD and over the Internet under the terms of the GPL.

2.2 The Evolution of "Free Software"

The Unix operating system was also developed on a cooperative basis by AT&T with the active support of many universities and research establishments. Many of the early Unix contributors were disappointed when AT&T began in the late 1970's and 1980's, to enforce their copyright terms over the use and distribution of Unix. This eventually resulted in the long and bitter legal battle between AT&T (and subsequently Novell who bought the Unix copyrights from AT&T in 1991) and the University of California at Berkeley. In a partial response to this problem of individual control of a public software development project, The Massachusetts Institute of Technology (MIT) in Cambridge, MA has, since 1984, supported Richard Stallman's efforts to launch a movement in the software development community to support the development of free software. This resulted in the establishment of The Free Software Foundation (the FSF), and its GNU project. The name GNU follows in an early Unix tradition of using recursive acronyms as program names, and stands for Gnu's Not Unix. The FSF continues to be head-quartered at MIT, and has enjoyed amazing success over the last decade with products like GNU C, GNU C++, Emacs, and many other products, many of which form substantial and key building blocks of the Linux operating system. Richard Stallman insists, with some justification, that Linux should correctly be known as a GNU system.

Also coming from MIT, but not related to the FSF or the GPL, is the X Consortium, which is a Unix industry sponsored effort to build and maintain the X Window System. In turn, a group called the XFree86 Project has taken on the responsibility to port the X Window System to the Intel platform. To keep the contributions of these two groups in context, of the approximately 200 MB of compressed source code in Red Hat Linux, roughly one third is FSF code and one third is X Consortium code. Linux is continuing to progress very rapidly because of the contributions of this world wide development effort, to which you and your company or school are encouraged to contribute.

2.3 The GNU Public License

The purpose of the GPL is much like any standard copyright license, to define what you can and cannot use the product for. However it differs substantially from commercial licenses because instead of restricting your use of the software its purpose is to *guarantee* your use of the software.

It in no way restricts the use of standard commercially licensed software with Linux or other GPL'd code. Only the changes that you make to the code that you "borrowed" from someone else that was licensed under the GPL must be made available to others under the same unrestricted rules defined by the GPL. Any product that simply uses or operates on top of Linux can be licensed under any commercial rules you chose.

There are many leading commercial software developers who are actively supporting their commercial products on Linux for which you must purchase a license, such as Motif from the OSF, Empress RDBMS from Empress Software, and recently WordPerfect, the word processor from Novell.

You will find a complete copy of the GPL in section **??**.

2.4 Will Linux Replace Commercial OSes?

While this is a pleasant thought that keeps many of us motivated, in reality the answer is: probably not. The company we know affectionately as the "Evil Empire", is too wealthy, and too clever a marketing organization to let such a thing happen.

On the other hand, the huge development effort and wide distribution of the Linux OS will ensure that it takes its place as a real, viable, and significant alternative to commercially restricted operating systems. The open development model, availability of source, and lack of license restrictions are "features" of the Linux OS that commercial OS developers simply cannot offer. Software development groups who need this model include groups from government affiliated research organizations, to academic research and teaching projects, to commercial software application developers.

The new distribution and development model that Linux, the FSF's GNU code, and other "freely distributable" software represent is a new model that is already successfully competing with the older commercially-restricted model. There is an exciting future for these technologies that we are pleased that you are now a part of.

2.5 Red Hat Software, Inc.'s Role in Linux Development

The Red Hat Linux distribution is also issued under the GPL. We see our role as making the Linux OS easy to install, configure, and maintain for professional developers, system administrators, and students. Red Hat Linux is available at no cost and few restrictions (see the GPL) on many ftp sites on the Internet. It is also available on CD from Red Hat Software (`http://www.redhat.com` or (800) 546-7274) and from most of the Linux archive CD vendors.

Red Hat Software, Inc. provides support for users of the Linux OS, from individuals running a single workstation to large organizations running hundreds of networked machines, in a variety of programs.

We gratefully acknowledge the support that we have received from the Linux development community including Linus Torvalds, everyone on the Linux contributors list, and the thousands of other developers who helped make Linux the success it is today. We would also like to acknowledge the growing contribution of commercial developers to our efforts including Digital Equipment Corporation, O'Reilly & Associates, Pacific Hi-Tech, and many others. You are encouraged to use Red Hat's Linux distribution, to develop and add features, or simply package programs that you need or that you think others would appreciate. Please do not hesitate to contact us for any help you require.

You can contact Red Hat Software directly at: *info@redhat.com*.

2.6 Further Reading

There are Internet based listings of both the freely distributable, and commercial software available for Linux in documents such as the Commercial HOWTO and the Linux Software Map, and from many Linux vendors, including Red Hat Software's retail division, the ACC Bookstore. Many third party and commercial products can be purchased through the catalog, including Motif, database development systems, editors, and more. A copy the catalog can be obtained by sending a fax request to (203) 454-2582, and can be browsed on the web at `http://www.redhat.com/acc`.

For more information on Linux please see:

- *Running Linux*, M. Welsh, O'Reilly & Associates, 1995.
- *Linux: Network Administrators Guide*, O'Reilly & Associates, 1995.
- `ftp://ftp.redhat.com/pub/`, `http://www.redhat.com/`
- The Free Software Foundation `ftp://prep.ai.mit.edu/pub/gnu`, `gnu@prep.ai.mit.edu`
- X Consortium, and XFree86, `http://www.x.org``http://www.xfree86.org`
- For general Unix questions, please see the full line of O'Reilly & Associates books. The are perhaps the best reference material for all things Unix related. They can be purchased from the Red Hat/ACC Online Catalog (`http://www.redhat.com/acc`).

Chapter 3

Hardware Requirements

All devices that have drivers in the standard Linux kernel are supported in the Red Hat kernel, with the exception of sound cards. The sound drivers require machine specific parameters to be configured at compile time, making it practically impossible to implement in a stock boot image. You can compile your own kernel with sound support after installation. For more info on how to do this, see the Kernel-HOWTO (which would be in `/usr/doc/HOWTO`).

For more info on special hardware that is supported by the kernel directly, including SCSI devices, see the Hardware-HOWTO and the SCSI-HOWTO (in the same place as above). There is an XFree86 HOWTO as well that lists supported video cards.

If you will be using a boot disk, a 1.44M floppy drive connected as the first physical floppy device (`a:`) is required. Here are the requirements for various popular combinations of software:

Minimum Text Based Installation

- 386sx or better CPU
- 4M RAM for Floppyless CD-ROM Install or Single Floppy CD-ROM Install
- 8M RAM for FTP, NFS or Floppy install
- 40M Hard Drive

- Any working video card (Hercules, CGA, VGA, SVGA, etc)
- Any supported CD-ROM drive

Minimum Text Based Installation, with X Window System

- 386sx or better CPU
- 4M RAM for Floppyless CD-ROM Install or Single Floppy CD-ROM Install
- 8M RAM for FTP, NFS or Floppy install
- 80M Hard Drive
- Any XFree86 Supported Video card (VGA, and SVGA, see below)
- Mouse (most types are supported)
- Any supported CD-ROM drive

Minimum X Based Installation

- 386sx or better CPU
- 8M RAM for Floppyless CD-ROM Install or Single Floppy CD-ROM Install
- 12M RAM for NFS install
- 80M Hard Drive
- Any XFree86 Supported Video Card (VGA, and SVGA, see below)
- Mouse (most types are supported)
- Any supported CD-ROM drive

Recommended Configuration

- 486dx or better CPU
- 16M RAM

- 300M Hard Drive
- Any XFree86 Supported SVGA Card
- 3 Button Mouse
- SCSI Tape Drive (Optional)
- UPS (Optional)
- Double Spin CD-ROM drive

Supported video cards include:

- Most Diamond Cards
- Most S3 Based Cards
- ET4000 Based Cards
- ATI Cards
- Cirrus Logic 542x and 543x
- Chips and Technologies Based Cards
- Trident 8900 and 9400
- Most #9 Cards

Supported CD-ROM drives include:

- All IDE/ATAPI Compliant Drives
- All SCSI Drives connected to a *supported* controller card
- All Sound Blaster Interface Drives (Matsushta/Kotobuki/Panasonic)
- Mitsumi Drives
- Sony 535, CDU 31, CDU 33

Chapter 4

Upgrading

Congratulations, you are about to perform the most painless system upgrade in the history of Linux. You *must* already have Red Hat Linux release 2.0 (or later) installed to do this upgrade. If you have an older version, or you or do not yet have Red Hat installed at all, your will need to do a complete installation as described in chapter 6.

If there is a `README` on your CD-ROM (or FTP site) please read it! It may contain new or updated information about the upgrade process.

4.0.1 The Upgrade Script

On the Red Hat CD-ROM (or FTP site) you will see a script called `upgrade`. This is a perl script which will analyze your installed system and the new Red Hat release to determine what packages need to be upgraded.

If you haven't done anything strange to your system you can just run the upgrade script as follows:

```
cd /mnt/cdrom
more README
./upgrade RedHat/RPMS/*.rpm
```

If you want to see what `upgrade` would do, read on...

Running Upgrade in Test Mode

The first thing you should do is run the script in `test mode` as follows:

```
cd /mnt/cdrom
./upgrade --test RedHat/RPMS/*.rpm
```

Running `upgrade` in this mode will *not* actually perform any upgrades – it just tells you what it *would* do.

You will first see something like:

```
Red Hat RPM system upgrader, version 0.1
Copyright (c) 1995 Red Hat Software

Finding packages...

Would run: rpm -Uvh rpm-1.4-1.i386.rpm
```

Upgrading RPM

If you are running an older version of rpm than the one listed, the rest of the `./upgrade --test` may not work properly. If you find that is the case, run the following to upgrade rpm:

```
rpm -Uvh /mnt/cdrom/RedHat/RPMS/rpm-*.i386.rpm
```

After upgrading `rpm`, you can run: `./upgrade --test RedHat/RPMS/*.rpm` again to see what the upgrade will do.

Test Mode Output

The output of the test mode will continue with something like:

```
Taking stock of things...

Packages installed:   128
Files installed   : 12709
```

```
Packages available:   308

Determining packages to upgrade...

Package              New Version          Old Version
====================================================
MAKEDEV              2.2-1                2.1-1
NetKit-A             0.08-4               0.08-2
NetKit-B             0.06-3               0.06-1
SysVinit             2.56-3               2.56-2
...
```

The "Taking stock of things..." section can take quite a while while as it analyzes your system.

The first list is a list of packages that are new (relative to the packages you have installed on your system already). A second list may be printed which will look similar to:

```
Files moved to                      Version
===========================================
texmf-dvips                         6.1-1
texmf-dvilj                         6.1-1
texmf-latex                         6.1-1
npasswd-dicts                       1.2-2
texmf                               6.1-1
NetKit-B-lpr                        0.06-3
...
```

This is a list of packages that contain file that appear to have moved from other packages. And finally, a third list may be printed:

```
Shared libs moved to                Version
===========================================
ncurses-devel                       1.9.6-1
```

The reason for this list is a little arcane. But in case you want to know, it lists packages that contains `new` versions of `shared` libraries that have been moved from other packages.

What Upgrade Will Do

After all that, the upgrade script will print a list of commands that it *would* be executed if you ran it without the `--test` option.

```
Upgrading packages...

Would run: rpm -Uvh RedHat/RPMS/MAKEDEV-2.2-1.i386.rpm
Would run: rpm -Uvh RedHat/RPMS/NetKit-A-0.08-4.i386.rpm
Would run: rpm -Uvh RedHat/RPMS/NetKit-B-0.06-3.i386.rpm
Would run: rpm -Uvh RedHat/RPMS/NetKit-B-lpr-0.06-3.i386.rpm
Would run: rpm -Uvh RedHat/RPMS/SysVinit-2.56-3.i386.rpm
Would run: rpm -Uvh RedHat/RPMS/XFree86-W32-3.1.2-1.i386.rpm
Would run: rpm -Uvh RedHat/RPMS/Xconfigurator-1.2-1.i386.rpm
Would run: rpm -Uvh RedHat/RPMS/abuse-0.34-2.i386.rpm
...
```

4.0.2 Performing the Upgrade

If after running the upgrade script in test mode, you think everything looks right (and it probably does), go ahead and run it without the `--test` option.

```
cd /mnt/cdrom
./upgrade RedHat/RPMS/*.rpm
```

If you do not agree with what the upgrade script would do, you can copy the "`Would run:  rpm -Uvh ...`" lines to a file, edit it to your liking, and run it as a shell script.

Chapter 5

Quick Start

This chapter tells you how to install Red Hat Linux if you are already experienced at Linux installations. If you don't understand this chapter, read the following one, which goes into much more detail.

5.1 Get Red Hat Linux

There are several ways to get Red Hat Linux. The best way to get it is on CD-ROM. This may not be practical for those of you who don't have CD-ROM drives, so we have made it freely available via FTP. You can get it from any of these Red Hat mirrors listed in chapter 13.

These sites are provided for those who want to install via FTP or want package upgrades. It is possible to download the distribution to a hard drive and install from there, but it is highly impractical for most and is beyond the scope of this document (it is covered in the RedHat-HOWTO, which is also available the Red Hat mirror sites).

To get the CD-ROM, contact Red Hat Software via any of the means listed in chapter 13.

5.2 Make Floppies

[Note: When you boot the Linux kernel during installation, it prompts you to insert a "ramdisk." A better term is "root disk," but we'll stick to "ramdisk" as long as that term appears in the kernel messages.]

If there is a README file on your CD-ROM (or on the FTP site), read it. It contains the latest information on your release, some of which may be different from what you are about to read.

See figure 6.2 and section 6.3.1 to determine the number of floppies required for your installation. If you elect the no floppy install skip ahead to section 5.4 to begin. If you are doing a one floppy install ignore the instructions for making ramdisks.

The `images` directory on the CD-ROM or the FTP site is the root of the boot disk images. Change to the `1213` directory. Read the `image.txt` file and choose a hardware configuration. Choose the boot image `bootXXXX.img` that corresponds to the image listed in the file. Use `dd` or `rawrite.exe` (found in the `dosutils` directory) to write the proper boot image file to a formatted high density (1.44Mb) 3.5 inch floppy.

Do the same for the two ramdisks, using the `images/ramdisk1.img` and `images/ramdisk2.img` images.

If you are creating these disks from an existing Linux system, just run `mkfloppies.pl` which will help your create your floppies.

5.3 Install With Boot Floppy

Insert the boot floppy into drive A, and insert the CD-ROM into your CD-ROM drive (for a CD-ROM install) or connect to your network (for an FTP or FS install). Then reboot, insert the ramdisks disk when asked, and answer all questions as they are presented.

5.4 Install without Floppies

If you have DOS installed on your computer and can access your CD-ROM from DOS you may be able to install Red Hat without using floppy disks. Put the Red Hat CD in your drive, make the CD-ROM drive the active drive and type `redhat`. You will go through an interactive image selection process and then Linux will attempt to boot.

5.5 Running Directly off the CD-ROM

If your Red Hat Linux CD-ROM came with a "live filesystem" you can run (with some limitations) Red Hat right off the CD-ROM without installing anything on your hard drive. This can be useful if you just wish to try out Red Hat or have a look at the graphical system administration tools. It can also be used as a learning environment for new Linux users, allowing them to become familiar with the environment and new commands without going through a complete installation.

If there is a README file on your Live Filesystem CD-ROM, read it. It contains the latest information on your CD-ROM, some of which may be different from what you are about to read. First, you need to create boot and ram disks. The `images` directory on the CD-ROM contains all the disk images. Section 6.3.1 explains how to select and create the proper boot disk for your hardware. The ramdisk image is `liveram.img`. Use `dd` or `rawrite` as described in section 6.3.1 to write `liveram.img` to your second floppy disk.

If you'd like to store some files between sessions, you may create a disk for `/home` by following the instructions at boot time. Be sure to have a blank floppy ready.

Now boot your system with the boot floppy (with the CD-ROM inserted), and insert the ram disk when prompted. The system will probe for your CD-ROM. If it does not find it you will need to reboot and enter parameters at the lilo boot prompt to force detection of your CD-ROM drive. See section 6.3.4 for or more details.

If you are going to use a `/home` floppy disk, insert it now. If it isn't already formatted, it will be formatted before being mounted at `/home`. While using the system, you can copy files to `/home` to save them.

If you are not using a `/home` floppy, type “n” and press enter.

When the login prompt appears login as `root`. To run X Windows (which you'll want to do so you can try the control panel and glint) first run `Xconfigurator` to configure X for your hardware. Chapter 7.2 describes the `Xconfigurator` and its use. To start X Windows type `startx`. You can now hack around to your heart's content!

To stop X Windows, type Control-Alt-Backspace. To shutdown the system, type `shutdown -h now`.

Chapter 6

Installation in Detail

Most people find the installation of Red Hat Linux to be painless. If all your hardware is configured properly, is compatible with Linux, and recognized at boot time, rest assured that the hard part is done!

6.1 Before You Begin

The first step in the install process is to obtain an up-to-date version of the Red Hat FAQ. The FAQ contains answers to Frequently Asked Questions and is the most current source of information on Red Hat Linux. You can obtain a copy of the Red Hat FAQ by sending email to:

```
faq@redhat.com
```

The subject line and message body are ignored and can be left blank. You can also get a current copy from our World Wide Web site by pointing your browser to:

```
http://www.redhat.com/RedHat-FAQ
```

If you will be connected to a network, be sure you know your IP address, network address, net mask, broadcast address, gateway IP address, and name server IP addresses. If you don't know these values, ask your network administrator for them.

If Linux will coexist on your machine with OS/2, you must create your partitions with the OS/2 partitioning software. This is vitally important. During the installation, do not create any new partitions, just set the types properly for your Linux partitions.

Please read all of the installation instructions *before* starting! This will prepare you for any decisions that need to be made and should eliminate any potential surprises.

6.2 Installation Methods

Depending upon your hardware and choice of installation method you will need from zero to four formatted 3.5 inch high density (1.44Mb) floppy disks to begin. Please choose your installation method carefully and keep in mind that while all methods will work for some hardware, and most methods will work for most hardware, there are hardware configurations that can only utilize one of the installation methods. Figure 6.1 should help you determine the best way to proceed with installation on your hardware. Regardless of the installation method, it is recommended that you make an appropriate boot disk, ramdisk1 and a rescue disk for your final system. These disks will allow you to recover from file system corruption and other mishaps that may occur. If you will be installing from a Red Hat CD you will most likely want to choose either the single floppy or floppyless install method. The single floppy install requires that you provide parameters at boot time, pressing F7 will bring up a help screen for these parameters.

Hardware	FTP	NFS	CD	Floppy	HD
RAM (Mb)	8	8	4	8	8
Network	X	X			
Floppy	X	X		X	X

Figure 6.1: Minimum Hardware Requirements

6.3 Starting the Installation

The installation instructions in this chapter are divided into three sections. This section applies to all installations. After finishing this section, you should continue with section 6.4 for X Windows based installs, or with section 6.5 for text based installs (including floppy and FTP installs).

If you are using the diskless install you can skip ahead to section 6.3.2 and proceed from there. Use figure 6.2 to determine which boot method you will use. The PCMCIA column is relevant only if you will be installing from a PCMCIA device.

Disks Used	FTP	NFS	CD	Floppy	HD	PCMCIA
0			X			
1			X			
3	X	X	X	X	X	X

Figure 6.2: Boot Disk Options

6.3.1 Creating Boot and Root Disks

You must first create a boot disk to use during the install. You will also need two ramdisks if you are not doing a CD or NFS rooted install. These must be 1.44 Mb 3.5 inch floppies. The disk images for these disks are located under the `images` directory on the CD or in the directory where you FTP'ed the distribution.

After changing to the `images` directory, change to the proper kernel version directory. The directory name for the kernel will be the version number with the periods removed (ie. kernel 1.2.34 would be in the directory `1234`). We recommend the use of images from the `1213` dierctory, because this is the current stable kernel version. `1.3.57` images are included to offer flexibility for users who have hardware that may not have been fully supported in version `1.2.13`. There are also additional images in the `custom` directory that have been built for various purposes since our last release. The `1.3.57` images and the `custom` images are provided as a *service* to our customers, Red Hat can only offer support on the current stable kernel version, (`1.2.13`).

Read the file `image.txt` and choose a configuration that matches your hardware as closely as possible. The only ambiguity here is the fact that there is an "Other" category of ethernet cards. This is the category that the NE-2000 and many other cards are in. If your card is supported under Linux and is not listed elsewhere, it should be in this category.

Please note that all images have support for ATAPI CD-ROM drives, and that a SCSI CD-ROM requires only SCSI support. All images support all mice, SLIP, CSLIP, PPP, FPU emulation, all file systems except extfs and xiafs, console selection, ELF, SysV IPC, IP forwarding, firewalling and accounting, reverse ARP, and parallel printers. (Note: PLIP is omitted in order to support parallel printers.)

None of the images have QIC tape support or sound card support. After the installation is complete you may want to rebuild a kernel that only includes support for your hardware. See section 7.9 for information on how to build a customized kernel.

Making Floppies Under DOS

After choosing a kernel configuration, write the corresponding boot image `bootXXXX.img` file to the first floppy disk and label it. You can do this using the `rawrite` command under DOS. You would execute the following command (assuming your CD is drive `d:`):

```
d:\dosutils\rawrite.exe
```

Rawrite will ask you for a filename. Enter the `bootXXXX.img` that you recorded earlier. It will then ask for a drive. This should always be `a:`. If you need to make ramdisks for the 3 disk install, cd up one level (`cd ..`) and run `rawrite` again. When prompted for a file name, enter `ramdisk1.img`. Again, enter `a:` for the drive name and continue. After this disk is finished, repeat the above steps with a new disk and enter `ramdisk2.img` as the image to write. You should now have three disks labeled `boot, ramdisk1, and ramdisk2`.

Making Floppies Under Linux

If you already have Linux installed, making your boot disks is really easy. Enter the the following commands (assuming you have mounted your CD-

ROM on /mnt/cdrom):

```
cd /mnt/cdrom/images
./mkfloppies.pl
```

The `mkfloppies.pl` script asks you about your hardware and makes the proper disks based on the answers. If possible, it also saves some of your configuration information such as network addresses and X configuration. You will then be prompted with those values as defaults during the install.

6.3.2 Floppyless Installation

To start the diskless install insert the Red Hat CD in your CD-ROM drive, make the CD-ROM the active drive and execute the following command (assuming, again, that your CD-ROM is drive `d:`

```
d:\redhat
```

A series of questions will be presented in order to determine which boot image is most suitable for your system. If you make an incorrect choice don't worry, you will have an opportunity to validate your hardware selections before the installation proceeds. The installation program will also ask you if you need to supply any boot parameters and make suggestions if some of your hardware requires parameters. If you are unsure accept the default parameters (which may be no parameters) and see how the install proceeds. If your system hangs or otherwise seems unstable after booting into linux see section 6.3.4 for some suggestions on boot parameters. After asking you to confirm the parameters the install will ask if you are ready to proceed and write a configuration file to the `c:` drive.

The floppyless install is only supported for the recommended images in the distribution. Development images, as well as images patched to support specific hardware, are not implemented in the diskless install. When the floppyless install boots go to section 6.3.6

6.3.3 Preparing for NFS, FTP, and Floppy Installs

NFS If you wish to install over a network, you will need to mount the RH Linux CD-ROM on a machine that supports ISO-9660 file systems with Rock Ridge extensions. The machine must also support NFS. Export the CD-ROM file system via NFS. You will need to know the NFS server's IP address and the path to the exported CD-ROM.

FTP For an FTP install, you must have a boot disk and two ramdisks. You will need to have a valid nameserver configured or the IP address of the FTP server you will be using. You will also need the path to the root of the Red Hat directory on the FTP site.

Floppy For a floppy install, you use the same boot disk and ramdisks as in the FTP install, but you also need to make approximately 100 floppies for a full install. You use the same method to make the floppies as you used to make the boot/ramdisks. You need to get the image files either from a CD, in images/floppies/ or via FTP and write them to their own floppies. There are a lot of floppies so it is important to label them well! It is also very important that you verify your floppies before using them. We recommend using new floppies only. One bad floppy can cause the entire install to go bad.

You need to get `main.img` and then each of the images from the directories for each series you want to install. For example, you need to get each of the images from the `Base` directory. If you want networking, you need to get all of the images from the `Networking` directory. Write each of these images to its own disk using the same method you used to write your boot/ramdisks.

To do the installation, just follow the instructions normally. The only noticeable difference (apart from speed), is that from time to time (especially during package installation) the installation script will ask you to insert a particular floppy disk.

Hard Drive To install Red Hat from a hard drive you will need the same boot and ramdisks used by the FTP install. You must first create a `RedHat` directory, everything you will install should be placed here. First copy the `base` subdirectory, then copy the packages you want to install to another subdirectory called `RPMS` You can use available space on an existing DOS partition or a Linux partition that is not required in the install procedure (for example, a partition that would be used for data storage on the installed system).

If you are using a DOS filesystem you will not be able to use the full Linux filenames for the `rpm` packages. The `RPM` utility does not care what the filenames look like, but it is a good idea that you keep track of them so you will know what you are installing.

6.3.4 Booting the Installation System

Boot your machine off the boot floppy you just created. You will first see the `boot:` prompt. The first time through, just press the Enter key. Watch the messages as the Linux kernel initializes your hardware. If the kernel boots and recognizes all of your hardware properly you are set! If it misses something or gets something wrong, you may need to enter some parameters at the `boot:` prompt, or use a different boot image. If you do need to specify some parameters, remember them! You will need them later.

6.3.5 Boot Disk Message

The message that is printed when you first boot the boot disk is:

```
                          Welcome to Red Hat Linux 3.0


You are at the boot prompt.  This is the first stage in getting Linux to
install on your machine.  In most cases, hitting Enter now will allow your
hardware to be detected.  If not, you either picked the wrong boot image
for your hardware, or you will need to enter boot parameters at the
prompt below.  If the former, please see your manual and try another boot
image.  If the latter, you can see the manual or get help on line.  For
on line help, use your function keys (F1, F2, etc) to get help on different
topics.  See the chart below for options:

        F1  - This Screen
        F2  - CD-ROM
        F3  - SCSI
        F4  - Ethernet
        F5  - Other Devices
        F6  - General Help
        F7  - Single Floppy Help
        F10 - Red Hat Ordering Information


[F1-Main] [F2-CD] [F3-SCSI] [F4-Ether] [F5-Other] [F6-Gen] [F7-Single]
boot:
```

Getting help for the boot parameters is as simple as pressing a `Function` key. The `boot:` prompt will remain at the bottom of the page, allowing you to enter parameters from different screens while keeping previous parameters right at the bottom of thescreen.

`F2` brings up perhaps the most important help screen, the CD-ROM screen. Failure to recognize the CD-ROM is the only problem that has the potential to cause real difficulty with the installation.

```
                        CD-ROM Help

The following drives may require the following parameters:

Mitsumi CD-ROM                      mcd=port,irq
Sony 31&33 CD-ROM REQUIRED          cdu31a=base_addr,[irq|0][,PAS]
Aztech CD268                        aztcd=port
SoundBlaster Pro or 16 compatible   sbpcd=io_addr,{SoundBlaster,Lasermate,SPEA}
ATAPI/IDE CD-ROM Drives             hd{a,b,c,d}=cdrom

Examples of the above would be:
boot: linux mcd=0x340,11          # A non-IDE Mitsumi on port 340, IRQ 11
boot: linux cdu31a=0x340,0        # A CDU 31 -or- 33 at port 340, no IRQ
boot: linux aztcd=0x220           # An Aztech CD-ROM at port 220
boot: linux hdc=cdrom             # IDE, master on second interface
boot: linux sbpcd=0x230,SoundBlaster
                                  # A Panasonic type CD-ROM at port 230

Note:  Most newer Sound Blaster cards come with IDE interfaces.  You do
NOT need to use an sbpcd image for those, a normal IDE image will work.
Also, don't use "sbpcd" parameters, only use hd* parameters.


[F1-Main] [F2-CD] [F3-SCSI] [F4-Ether] [F5-Other] [F6-Gen] [F7-Single]
boot:
```

Here is a close examination of each line in the CD-ROM help message:

- Lines 1-3: Descriptive information.
- Line 5: Use this if your Mitsumi CD-ROM does not get recognized properly. Example: `linux mcd=0x340,11`

- Line 6: This line is required for the sony cdu31a or 33a. Use "cdu31a" for BOTH the 31 and the 33 (ie. do NOT use "cdu33a" as a parameter on the command line). An example: `linux cdu31a=0x340,0`
- Line 7: If you have an Aztech CD268, try: `linux aztcd=0x340` (or whatever your port is).
- Line 8: If you have an IDE (ATAPI compliant) CD-ROM that is not getting recognized by the autoprobe, you can use this parameter to tell it where to look. Normally, if you have IDE hard drives, they take up the first available drive letters. If you had 2 IDE hard drives, your CD-ROM would be hdc. If you had one IDE hard drive, it would be hdb. It's usually okay to just try them all. You would use: `linux hdb=CD-ROM` if you had one IDE hard drive.
- Line 9: Use this if you have the "normal" Sound Blaster CD interface and it doesn't work. This is the regular run-of-the-mill Sound Blaster type that controls the Panasonic 56x drives, Matsushta Kotobuki drives, TEAC CD55A, and a few others. If you have a Sound Blaster with something like the Panasonic connected using base address 0x240, you would use: `linux sbpcd=0x240,SoundBlaster`

Pressing `F3` will bring up the SCSI help screen;

```
                              SCSI Help

The format of the SCSI params are as follows:

SCSI Seagate ST0x                     st0x=base_addr,irq
SCSI Future Domain TMC-8xx            tmc8xx=base_addr,irq
SCSI Trantor T128                     t128=base_addr,irq
SCSI NCR-5380 Based                   ncr5380=port,irq,dma_channel
Adaptec 15{1,2}x, SoundBlasterSCSI    aha152x=port,irq,scsi_id,reconnect,parity
Adaptec 1542                          aha1542=base_addr
Buslogic                              buslogic=base_addr
Pro Audio Spectrum / Studio 16        pas16=port,irq

Some examples would be:

      boot: linux aha1542=0x330
      boot: linux aha152x=0x330,11,7
```

```
        boot: linux tmc8xx=0x330,11

Note, the above are verbose.  For an AHA1522, use "aha152x".  For an
AHA1505, use "aha152x".  For a TMC800, use "tmc8xx".


[F1-Main] [F2-CD] [F3-SCSI] [F4-Ether] [F5-Other] [F6-Gen] [F7-Single]
boot:
```

Here is a close examination of each line in the SCSI help message:

- Lines 1-3: Descriptive information.
- Line 5: For an old Seagate ST0x controller, use this parameter.
- Line 6: For a Future Domain TMC-8xx controller, use this parameter.
- Line 7: For a trantor T128, use this line.
- Line 8: For an NCR-5380, use this line. For a card at 0x330 and IRQ 11 and DMA 5, you would use: `linux ncr5380=0x330,11,5`
- Line 9: Use this line for an Adaptec 1505, 1510, 1515, 1520, and 1522 (and Sound Blaster SCSI). The reconnect and parity are optional. For a CD-ROM hooked to ID 1 an a controller with base address of 0x330 and IRQ 11 you would use:

  ```
  linux aha152x=0x330,11,1,reconnect,parity
  ```

  (you can try it without the last two)
- Line 10: Use this if you are having problems with an Adaptec 1542 (rare).
- Line 11: Use this if you are having trouble with a Buslogic controller (also rare).
- Line 12: Use this for Pro Audio Spectrums and Pro Audio Studio cards that aren't recognized.
- When a parameter has commas, make sure you do not put a space after a comma. The only spaces on the command line should be after `linux` and between multiple parameters (eg. `linux mcd=0x340,11 bmouse=5`).

The Ethernet Help screen (F4) contains the following information:

```
                         Ethernet Help

The format of the ethernet parameter is as follows:

        ether=irq,base_addr,mem_start,mem_end

This shouldn't be necessary for many cards, however.  An example
might look like:

        boot:  linux ether=11,0x360

Note:
The last two parameters can be left out most (if not all) of the time.
Also, linux will only recognize the first ethernet card in a system.
To get it to see two, you must use something like:

        boot:  linux ether=0,0,eth1

For more information on that, see the Multiple-Ethernet mini HOWTO.



[F1-Main] [F2-CD] [F3-SCSI] [F4-Ether] [F5-Other] [F6-Gen] [F7-Single]
boot:
```

A detailed examination of this screen would be redundant, as well as the next.

The Other Devices Help screen (F5) contains the following information:

```
                     Miscellaneous Devices

If you have a bus mouse, you may need to specify the IRQ of the
interface card before the kernel will recognize it.  To do so,
you would enter:

boot: linux bmouse=IRQ
```

```
Where "IRQ" is the number of the interrupt your card is on.  Most cards
use something in the 2 through 5 range.



[F1-Main] [F2-CD] [F3-SCSI] [F4-Ether] [F5-Other] [F6-Gen] [F7-Single]
boot:
```

The General Help Screen (F6) contains the following information, which is covered here but presented at boot time for quick reference.

```
                          General Help

There are several great sources of help.  If you don't have a manual
or it doesn't address your problem, the first thing you should get is
the most up to date version of the RedHat-FAQ.  It can be found on:

        http://www.redhat.com

or you can get an ASCII version by sending mail to faq@redhat.com.
You should receive an autoreply within minutes.

Another great source of help is the redhat-list mailing list.  See our
WWW site above for more info on how to join.

For those without a manual, you can get the RedHat-HOWTO for free or
you can order our 150 page printed manual directly from us.  See our
WWW site for info on both of these.  You can also get ordering info
by pressing F10 now.



[F1-Main] [F2-CD] [F3-SCSI] [F4-Ether] [F5-Other] [F6-Gen] [F7-Single]
boot:
```

The Single Floppy help screen (F7) is very helpful as well. It provides important information for specifying the parameters you need to enter to make a single floppy install work.

```
                        Single Floppy Instructions

If you are installing using a CD-ROM, you can install using a boot
floppy only.  Use the chart below to find out what the proper parameter
should be for your device.  Then enter it below like the example.

IDE:
        hda                    /dev/hda    Sony 535                   1800
        hdb                    /dev/hdb    CDU 31 or 33               0F00
        hdc                    /dev/hdc    Aztech                     1D00
        hdd                    /dev/hdd    Phillips CM206             2000
SCSI                           0B00        Goldstar                   1000
Sound Blaster (non-IDE)        1900        Mitsumi (non-IDE)          1700

Example:
          boot:  linux root=/dev/hdc ramdisk=256
This will work for cases where your CD-ROM is autodetected.  If it isn't,
you may need something like:
          boot:  linux root=/dev/hdc hdc=cdrom ramdisk=256
Both of these examples are assuming your CD-ROM is /dev/hdc.  Substitute
values accordingly for your device.  Also, any other parameters you
may need can be added to the end of this line.

[F1-Main] [F2-CD] [F3-SCSI] [F4-Ether] [F5-Other] [F6-Gen] [F7-Single]
boot:
```

This screen is fairly self explanatory. Depending on your hardware configuration you need to enter parameters as shown above. For all single floppy installs you should use the `ramdisk=256` parameter. You also need a `root` option depending on your device. You may or may not need the `hdX=cdrom` option.

The final help screen (`F10`) contains information on how to obtain current information on Red Hat products as well as ordering and contact information.

After typing any required parameters press `ENTER` to begin the install process. If you are using the single disk install the next paragraph does not apply (because you are not using ramdisks). When you see the "VFS: Insert ramdisk floppy ..." message, insert the ramdisk1 floppy and press Enter. After a minute or so, you will be prompted for the ramdisk2 disk. Insert it and press Enter. If all goes well you will be presented with the welcome dialog box.

6.3.6 Using the Dialog Boxes

Use of the dialog boxes is quite simple. In most dialog boxes there is a "cursor" or "highlight bar" which you can move around with your arrow keys and the Tab key. If you are presented with a menu of items from which you are supposed to select one, move the highlight bar over the item you wish to select, and press Enter. If you are presented with a list of items and you are supposed to select any number of items (a *checklist*) move the highlight bar and press the space bar to select an item. To deselect an item, press the space bar again. Press Enter when you have finished selecting items. A word of warning - do not press random keys during the installation process. This may result in unpredictable behavior.

6.3.7 Boot Floppy

When the installation script loads the opening screen will be in black and white. You will be asked if you have a color display, if you answer 'Yes' the install will continue in color. If you used ramdisks you will be asked to insert the boot disk. Remove the second ramdisk and insert the original boot disk, then press Enter.

6.3.8 Installation Type

If you are doing a 3 floppy install you will now be offered a choice of five installation methods. If you are doing a floppyless or single floppy install this step is skipped.

CD-ROM If you have a CD-ROM drive with the Red Hat CD.

NFS If you have an NFS server with the Red Hat CD (or a mirror).

Local Hard Drive If you copied the Red Hat files to one of your hard drives.

FTP If you want to install directly from an FTP server.

Floppy Disks If you are installing via floppy disks.

If you select CD-ROM or NFS type installs, you will be asked if you want to do an X based (graphical) or text based install. Both installation methods offer the ability to choose components on a package-by-package basis. The text install will provide a summary of required disk space and run faster than the graphical installation. The X install is a bit more intuitive and offers a point-and-click interface.

If the X install fails, you can always drop back and do the text install. The other three install methods require a text based install.

6.3.9 Disk Partitions

For those who are not familiar with hard drive partitioning this section contains invaluable information. A hard drive has a large platter that can hold lots of data, however it is not organized in any particular way when it comes from the factory. There is now a partition table standard for hard drives that allows us to take a hard drive and make it look like several containers for data instead of one large container. If you bought your machine with DOS preloaded on it, you probably have one large partition. Changing the partition size is *bad* if you have data you don't want to lose. Always keep in mind that you can change your partition table without losing data, but *only* if you do not alter the size of the partitions that you don't want to lose. This means if you have a single DOS partition on your only drive, you are in a bit of trouble. Luckily, there is a program called `fips`. `fips` will allow you to resize an existing DOS partition without losing the data that is there. You must run the `defrag` program that comes with DOS 6.2 (or something equivalent) first. You will find `fips` in the `dosutils` directory on the CD. We cannot recommend its use without insisting you back up your DOS data first, however. We have not heard of it losing data, but your data is a serious matter and should be backed up.

Red Hat Linux *must* have its own partition to be installed to. It is also a good idea to create a partition for swap space. If you have 16 Mb or less you must create and use a swap partition. For decent basic performance, you should have at least 24 Mb of combined RAM and swap space.

If you plan to *really* use Linux, you'll want to divide your system over two or more partitions. That option is discussed below. You can create these partitions with the `fdisk` utility that comes with any operating system.

As mentioned in the beginning of this chapter, if OS/2 and Linux will be sharing a hard drive, you *must* create your partitions with the OS/2 `fdisk`. If you fail to partition with the OS/2 `fdisk` your disk may be totally unusable to OS/2.

There is a fundamental part of the partitioning process that you *must* get right. You must tag your partitions properly. When you use `fdisk` to create your partitions, each new partition will have a default type of `Linux Native`. This is fine for all Linux partitions, but you will need to change it for your swap partition. You need it to be partition type 82, or `Linux Swap`. Even if you create your partitions with some other software (ie. the OS/2 `fdisk`), you must still use the Linux `fdisk` to tag the partitions to the proper type.

The next screen lets you choose between `fdisk` or `cfdisk`. It is recommended that you use `cfdisk`, and only resort to `fdisk` if `cfdisk` gives you problems. Select the one you want to use with the arrow keys and press Enter.

A list of drives found on your system is then displayed. Select a drive to partition. After partitioning that drive you will be offered the chance to partition another drive.

We recommend a configuration such as:

- If you have 8M of RAM, make a 16-24M swap partition (depending on how much you plan to do with Linux at one time). If you have 16M or more of RAM, just make as much swap as you have RAM.
- Make a 30M `/` partition
- Make a 150M (or more depending on how much you want to install) `/usr` partition. If you plan to install everything, this should be more like 350M.
- If you plan to install a lot of the source (which is not required), you may want to make a `/usr/src` partition as well of about 200M.
- Make a 50M or so `/home` partition. This is where all user's home directories go, so you are completely at your own discretion on size for this one (although 50M is a good number for a single user system, 200M may be too much for a 4 user system).

- You may want a 50M or so `/usr/local` partition as well for software that doesn't come from RPM's.

While creating partitions, it is a good idea to write down which partitions are meant for which file systems.

Creating different partitions allows you to more easily back up your data and will also allow you to move your data around more easily should you need to increase partition sizes. If you are using a lot of source, it's much easier to move 200M of stuff somewhere else, repartition, and move it back than it is to move a 600M root partition somewhere!

After exiting the partitioning program, if you see a message like "Re-read table failed with error ..." you will need to reboot your machine so that Linux can reload the partition table data. This generally happens if you create, change, or delete any extended partitions. If you need to reboot, do so, and go through all the same steps you did to get to the partitioning step, but then skip the partitioning step (you've already done it).

Once you are done partitioning, the installation will probe for swap partitions. If it does find one, it will ask you if you want to initialize it. It is a very good idea to do so now.

6.3.10 Configure Networking

Choose "Yes" if you have an ethernet card and wish to have that card activated at boot time. Choose "No" if you have a stand alone machine or network only over a serial line via PPP or SLIP.

If you choose "No", you can skip this section and go on to the next one.

If you choose "Yes", you will be presented with several menus to install networking. You will need to know several network parameters for your machine. Sometimes defaults will be provided. Figure 6.3 below lists the parameters that are requested and some example values. *These are only examples!! Do not use these parameters!!*

After entering the parameters, you will have the opportunity to review them and change them before committing to them.

Parameter	Example
Hostname	elroy
Domain Name	redhat.com
FQDN	elroy.redhat.com
IP Address	199.183.24.5
Network Address	199.183.24.0
Network Mask	255.255.255.0
Broadcast Address	199.183.24.255
Default Gateway	199.192.24.1
Nameserver	199.183.24.101

Figure 6.3: Sample Networking Parameters

6.3.11 Setup Media

Note: If you are doing the floppyless or single floppy install, this step is skipped because you must be doing a CD-ROM install.

CD-ROM Install At this point, the CD-ROM devices are probed in an attempt to find the Red Hat media. If all goes well, one will be found and the CD will be mounted. If it fails, that means one of several things could have gone wrong:

- You picked the wrong boot image and the one you are using doesn't have support for your particular CD-ROM. In this case, you'll need to go back to DOS and remake your boot disk using a more appropriate image.
- You picked the right boot image, but for some reason the kernel didn't detect your hardware. In this case, you'll need to reboot and then specify hardware parameters.
- You have a SCSI CD-ROM and your controller card was not recognized properly. This could be due to having the wrong boot image or due to the need for hardware parameters at the LILO prompt.
- You forgot to insert the CD-ROM in the drive.

NFS Install If you haven't configured networking already, you must do so now. After that, you will be prompted for a server and a mount point. It's a good idea to use IP addresses for the server, but if you have configured a good nameserver with your networking, a hostname should work. You will then need to enter the mount path. If all goes well, your media will be mounted and you can continue at section 6.5. If the mount fails, you either configured networking wrong, or your server is refusing to allow you to mount. Try to make sure networking is correct, and then make sure you can mount the server from another machine.

FTP Install If you pick the FTP install, you will be presented with a list of known FTP sites. Try one of these sites or use your own by selecting "Other" and entering your own site. In this case, you will have to know the path to the RedHat directory.

At this point, you can continue with section 6.5.

Floppy Install You will be prompted to insert the "main" disk out of the floppy series. This disk is used to find out series information, etc. Once you are done, you can continue with section 6.5.

Local Hard Drive Install You will now be asked to enter the device where your Red Hat files are stored on your hard drive. You also must enter the filesystem type (ie. "msdos" for DOS filesystems, etc). Once you enter this and your files are found, you can continue to section 6.5.

6.3.12 Continuing the Install

If you are doing a text, FTP, local hard drive, or floppy install, continue with section 6.5.

If you are doing an X install, continue by reading the following section (section 6.4).

6.4 Graphical Installation

To do the graphical install, you first have to configure X for your system. If you use the Metro-X server the installation routine will use the `configX.ncurses` utility. See section 7.3 for details. If you use the XFree86 X server you can follow the instructions for X Configuration in section 7.2. Please note that if `Xconfigurator` doesn't properly configure

X, you can *not* use `xf86config`. You will have to go back and do the text based install instead, and then configure X with `xf86config` when you get your machine installed and rebooted.

You may have to wait a minute or two for X to start depending on your network or your CD-ROM speed. If X starts properly, you will get a screen with a window in the upper left asking you to press a button if everything looks OK. If it does, click on the button. Otherwise, you can wait for it to time out (it takes 30 seconds), or you can press Control-Alt-backspace to kill X windows. At that point, you can try to configure X again, or you can do the text install.

6.4.1 Choosing Partitions

If you have only one partition of type "Linux native", you will see a window telling you that since you have only one mountable partition it will use that for your root filesystem.

If you have more than one partition of type "Linux native", you will be presented with a menu of options like Figure 6.4, from which you need to select a "root partition." The root partition is where you store the root (`/`) filesystem. Select the root partition by clicking on it. Then click the "Done" button.

6.4.2 Selecting Partitions

You will be presented with a list of partitions on your system. For each partition you want to mount, select it with your mouse and click "Edit". This will bring up another window like the one in Figure 6.5 that will let you define a mount point for it (eg: `/usr`). Type in the mount point, including the leading "`/`".

6.4.3 Formatting Partitions

The next step asks you which partitions you would like to format. The window will be similar to Figure 6.6. It is highly recommended that you format all partitions on to which you plan to install RHL. None are selected

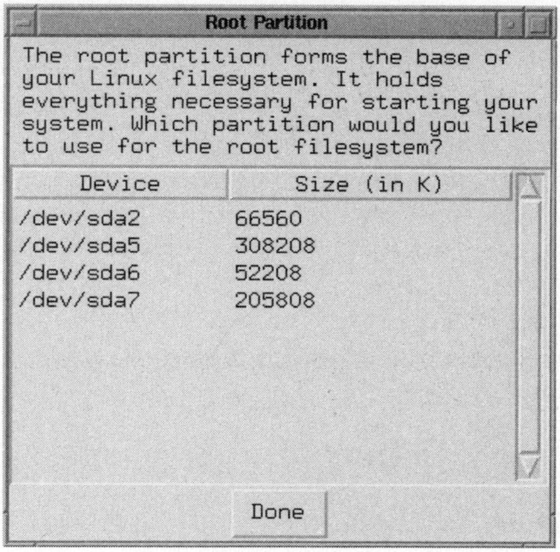

Figure 6.4: Root Filesystem Selection

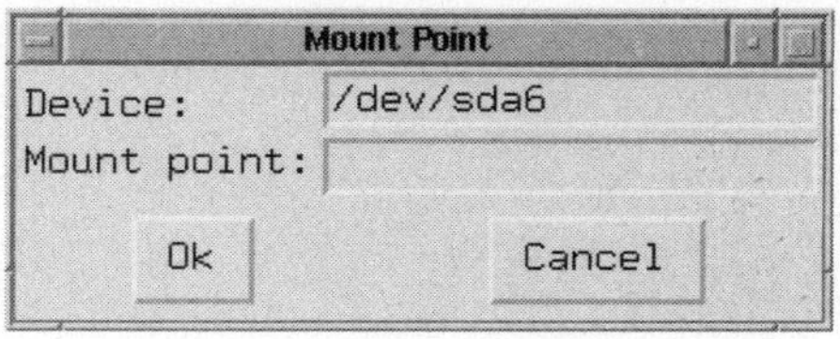

Figure 6.5: Edit Mount Point

by default to insure that you don't accidently format partitions that you may not have meant to.

If you have partitions from a previous Linux system that you wish to preserve (like a `/home` partition), do not select them. If you do select them, they will be formatted and you will lose your data!

Click the mouse button on each partition you want to format (this will result in it being highlighted). Then click the "Done" button. You will see a series of small windows indicating that your partitions are being formatted.

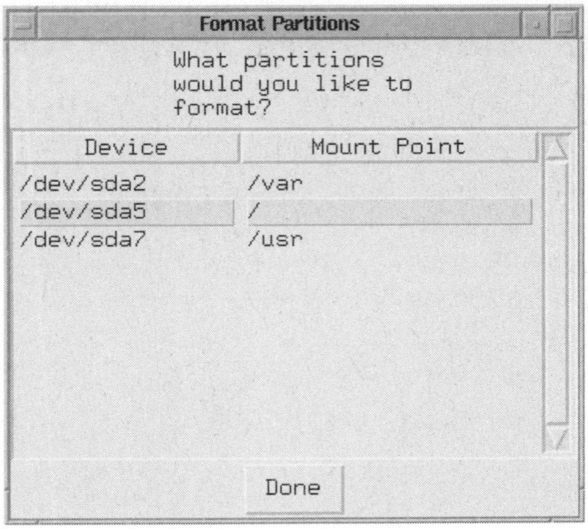

Figure 6.6: Format Partitions

6.4.4 Select Packages

You are now at the point where you select your software packages. A window is displayed (figure 6.7) that will let you select some software in groups. Selecting everything here *does not* select everything in the RHL system. Once you pick the groups you want, you will be presented with a window that looks much like a file manager (figure 6.8). You will see some folders with numbers and the occasional "All" printed on the folder. This tells you how many packages are selected in the folder. The bottom of the window tells you the disk space requirements for all the selected packages.

To select or unselect packages, simply click on the folder you want to change. Then find the package you want to select/deselect and click on it. Make sure you have more available disk space than you have selected packages.

You can move around in the package selection window much like a file manager. Double click on folders to open them, and double click on the "Back" folder to go back up a level. To select and deselect packages, simply click on them. You can see the disk space requirement at the bottom of the window change as you select and deselect packages (see figure 6.9 for an example of actual selected packages).

Your right mouse button creates a pop-up menu when pressed over a folder

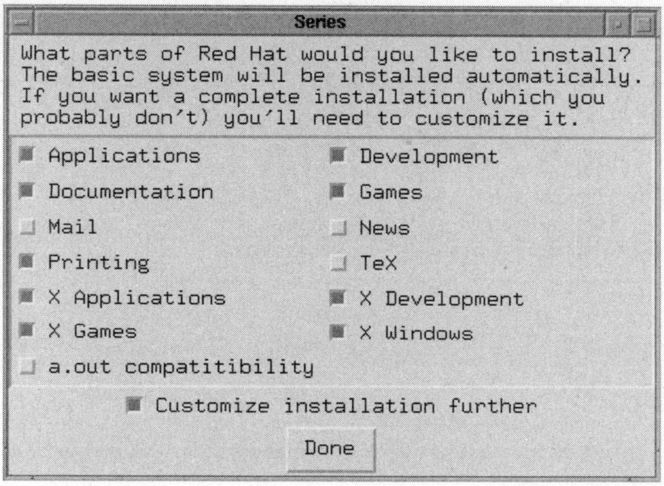

Figure 6.7: Series Selection

or a package. This menu allows you to select and unselect folders or packages, but it also allows you to "query" individual packages. If you query a package, you are given a window that lists the package name, description, and the file list. You can also select or unselect the package from here, as well as get more details such as who built the package, and when they did it, by pressing "Details" button. This works as well for folders of packages, except that the resulting window will give you a list on the left of all the packages and you can flip through all of them in the query window.

You can do the same "querying" using the button on the right of the main install window. This button will query *all* selected packages.

Once you have selected all the packages you want, click the "Install" button on the main window. A dialog box with two bar graphs displays the current state of the package installation. The top bar represents the current package being installed, and the bottom bar represents all packages being installed. Also shown are the package numbers, total kilobytes installed, and an estimated time for the install.

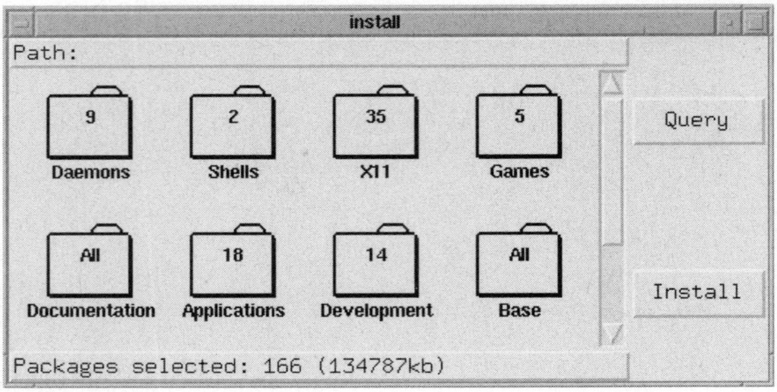

Figure 6.8: Main Customization Window

6.4.5 Finishing Up

After you've selected the packages and they are all installed, there are just a few more steps to do. You first need to indicate which time system you want to use. UTC is the international standard, and if you use it your machine will handle daylight saving properly, and moving from time zone to time zone will be a breeze. If you will be connected to a network, you should use UTC. Otherwise, Local Time is fine.

After that, you will need to select your time zone. Just click on the zone you are in. Then you select your keyboard mapping from the available list. Users in the United States, for instance, will choose `us.map`.

Then you'll need to install LILO, the LInux LOader. LILO is a small program that lets you choose between different operating systems when your computer boots. A window asks you where you want to install it. For most people, this is on the MBR of their first physical hard drive. You can also specify other operating systems for lilo to use. Once you've answered all the questions, you should be presented with a `lilo.conf` for reviewing. Hopefully, the worst thing that will happen is that Linux is the only operating system you can boot. If this happens, you can read the LILO-FAQ in `/usr/doc/FAQ` to find out how to fix lilo to boot other operating systems (such as DOS).

That should be it...you should be ready to reboot. Skip the following sections and go the section on "Rebooting" (section 6.6).

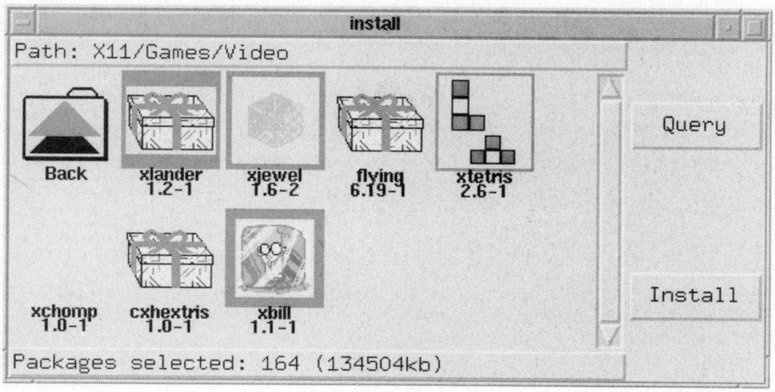

Figure 6.9: Choosing Packages

6.5 Continuing a Text Install

6.5.1 Select Filesystems for Format

You will now be presented with a list of partitions to format. Use the arrow keys and the space bar to select all the partitions you need to format. Do not select partitions that contain data you want to keep.

6.5.2 Mount Filesystems

You now need to select which filesystems to mount and where. You should be presented with a list of all partitions that were tagged as "Linux Native". You need to select "Add", and then select one of the partitions to use for a root partition. Continue adding partitions if necessary (if you are mounting in a separate `/usr` etc).

You may not be prompted with this step at all if you only have one partition of type "Linux Native" since that must be the one to use.

6.5.3 Kernel Installation

After the packages have installed, the install program will copy the kernel from the boot floppy to your new Linux system. This will take about a minute on most systems.

6.5.4 Package Installation

Series Selection

At this point, you must select the groups of software you want to install. You do so by moving the highlight bar with the arrow keys to the item you want to select and press the Space Bar on that item. When you have everything checked that you want, press Enter.

Package Selection

After you have selected the various series that you want to install you will be given the opportunity to customize your selections on a package-by-package basis. If you are unsure whether or not a package is needed it is better to install everything in question.

The package selection screen will indicate the total disk space required to install the selected packages at the top of the screen. A list of packages is presented on the screen in the following format;

```
Series Name          Required Space          Series Description
```

To customize a series highlight it with the arrow keys and press `Enter`. This will bring up a menu of the packages within the series and allow you to select specific packages for installation. The individual package screen will present a display in the format;

```
Package Name          Package Size          Package Description
```

As you make changes to the package selections the total at the top of the screen will change accordingly. When you have made all the changes you plan to, select `Finished` to start installing packages.

6.5.5 Mouse Configuration

Just pick the one from the list that matches your hardware. If you have a serial mouse, you will next select which serial (COM) port to use.

6.5.6 Network Configuration

If you are doing an NFS or FTP install, networking should already be configured at this point. You will be asked if you want to use those parameters for your installed system. If for some reason you do not want to use those parameters (for instance, if your machine is normally connected to another network, or not connected at all), you will have the opportunity to reconfigure networking. These parameters are not for SLIP/PPP connections.

If you are doing a CD-ROM, floppy, or hard drive install, and you want networking, you will need to configure networking now. See section 6.3.10 on how to configure networking properly, then return here.

Otherwise, just answer "No" when asked if you want to install networking and continue.

6.5.7 Modem Configuration

If you have a modem, you must tell the system which serial (COM) port it is on. This step simply makes a link from `/dev/modem` to the proper device under Linux so that programs like minicom will work with little configuration.

6.5.8 Clock Configuration

Next you will be asked if you want to use Local Time or GMT/UTC style time. UTC is the international standard, and if you use it your machine will handle daylight saving properly, and moving from time zone to time zone will be a breeze. If you will be connected to a network, you should use UTC. Otherwise, Local Time is fine.

After picking that, you will be asked for your time zone. Scroll through the list (using the arrow keys) until you find your time zone and then press Enter.

6.5.9 Select Keymap

For most systems, just press Enter. If you do not use a U.S. style keyboard, move the highlight bar (using the arrow keys) to the type you are using and press Enter.

6.5.10 LILO Installation

You should install LILO to boot your Linux system, unless you do not want to overwrite your MBR and you have another way to boot your Linux system. Installing LILO is quite safe and is recommended.

If you choose to install LILO, you are asked where you want to install LILO on your hard drive. On most systems, you will want to install to the MBR of the first physical disk. Some people using "Boot Manager" from OS/2 or something similar might want to install LILO to the superblock of the root partition.

Next you will be asked if you need to specify hardware parameters. If you had to type something at the `LILO boot:` prompt to get your system to install properly, you will probably want to put that here. Otherwise, select "No". If you select "Yes", type the parameters in the next window and press Enter.

Next you will be asked if you want to boot another operating system from LILO. If you do, answer "Yes". If not, answer "No". If you answered "Yes", you must now specify what type of partition to use. Continue by telling it what exactly you want to boot.

6.5.11 Creating User Accounts

If you want to start with some user accounts, create them now. It is recommended that you create a user account for yourself. To add a user, you first enter an account name. This must be a single "word" with no spaces, and ideally should be limited to 8 characters. As an example "djb" is a good account name. You have the option of *not* creating a home directory for the user. If you have an existing `/home` partition, or if you will be mounting `/home` over NFS, you may not want a `/home` directory to be created.

The user accounts that you create here will have their passwords "locked", preventing those users from logging in. To enable those accounts you must log in as root and run `passwd <account>` to set a password for each account.

6.5.12 Root Password

Enter your root password here. At all costs, make it something you will remember. Your password will need to mix numerals and upper and lower case characters.

You are finished! Continue with section 6.6.

6.6 Rebooting Your Machine

Once the installation is completed, you will be presented with the option to reboot the machine. Remove the disks from the floppy drive (otherwise, the system will boot from the floppy disk), and reboot. Provided everything went well and you installed LILO, you should get a `LILO boot:` prompt. Here you can do several things:

- Press Enter to boot the default OS (linux)
- Press Tab to see a list of possible OS's to boot
- Type the name of an alternate OS (like "dos").

The operating system you select will be booted.

Chapter 7

Post Installation Configuration

After installation your system is fully functional, but you may still want to do some additional configuration. This chapter describes some of the various system configuration tasks you may need to do.

7.1 Package Installation (or Uninstallation)

Remember that even if you selected every series available, there are still software packages on the CD-ROM that are not installed on your system. You can use rpm or glint to install additional packages. See chapters 9 and 11 for introductions to rpm and glint, respectively.

7.2 X Window Configuration with XFree86

There are three methods for configuring XFree on your machine: `Xconfigurator`, `xf86config`, or by hand. None of them are foolproof, and each them will do a better job that the others for some combinations of hardware. Unfortunately, that is the state of XFree configuration for Linux – you just have to try it and see if it works. If you are unsure of anything in this process, a good source of extra documentation is `http://www.xfree86.org`.

`Xconfigurator` is a full-screen menu driven program that walks you through the setup. `xf86config` is a line oriented program distributed with XFree86. It isn't as easy to use as `Xconfigurator`, but it usually works in cases where the latter fails. If both fail, you may have an unsupported card or you may need to write the config file by hand. Usually the former is the case, so check and make sure your card is supported before attempting to write the config file yourself. If your card is unsupported by XFree86 you will probably want to consider using a commercial X server, such as the Metro Link X server included with the Official Red Hat CD package.

All of this is moot, however, if you did the X based install. The X based install copies the config file that it used to your installed system. You should be able to reboot from the X install, login, and run `startx`.

7.2.1 The X Server

Provided you selected the proper chip-set type at install time, you should have the proper X server installed and linked in. When later running `Xconfigurator` or `xf86config`, you need to make sure you select this same chip-set or the autoprobe will fail.

If you think you installed the wrong X server for your chip-set, you will have to install the right one before you can configure it. To do so, execute the following commands (assuming the Red Hat CD-ROM is mounted on `/mnt/cdrom`, and that you need to install the S3 server):

```
cd /mnt/cdrom/RedHat/RPMS
rpm -ivh XFree86-S3-3.1.2-1.i386.rpm
ln -sf /usr/X11R6/bin/XF86_S3 /usr/X11R6/bin/X
```

This will install the S3 server and make the proper link.

7.2.2 Xconfigurator

`Xconfigurator` is simple to use, although it does require a little knowledge on your part. You will need to know what type of chip-set your card has. For example, most newer Diamond cards use the S3 chip-set, so you would want to install the S3 server for those. An ET4000, however, would use the generic SVGA server.

Selecting your Server

If you are unsure what chip-set you have, the best way to find out is usually to look at the card itself. This is unnecessary in most cases, but sometimes it is the only way. Figure 7.1 lists which chip-sets and boards require which servers. Pick the one that best matches your hardware.i

Server	Chip-set
VGA16	All VGA boards with 256K (16 color only)
SVGA	Trident 8900 & 9400, Cirrus Logic, C & T, ET4000, Others
Mach8	ATI boards using the Mach8 chip-set
Mach32	ATI boards using the Mach32 chip-set
Mach64	ATI boards using the Mach64 chip-set
8514	IBM 8514/A Boards and true clones
S3	#9 Boards, most Diamonds, some Orchids, Others
AGX	All XGA graphics boards
P9000	Diamond Viper (but not the 9100) and Others
W32	All ET4000/W32 cards, but not standard ET4000's

Figure 7.1: X Servers

Selecting your Mouse

This is fairly self explanatory. Just pick the one that matches your hardware.

Finishing Up

The Xconfigurator does something called an autoprobe, which tries to figure out what your hardware is and choose the right configuration options. From here, you should be able to just autoprobe and have everything else you need detected. If this fails, you'll need to run `xf86config`. You'll know this failed if you are asked questions that you don't know the answer to.

These questions are usually things like "Please enter your clocks" or "Which ramdac do you have".

Assuming everything goes fine for your card, you will be asked to select a monitor. There are many monitors in our database, but not *every* monitor. If your monitor isn't listed, you should pick "Generic Monitor" or "Generic Multisync". The former is for straight VGA resolution monitors, the latter for monitors that do up to 1024x768. You may find Generic Multisync lacking because it only does 1024x768 in interlaced mode. This is for protection to make sure you don't accidentally select something that could damage your monitor.

If later you want to increase your refresh rate for your monitor, you can edit the config file by hand or you can run `Xconfigurator` again and pick a monitor from our list that more closely matches the specs of your monitor.

Once the monitor is selected, you will be asked which video modes you would like to use. Here you can select multiple modes using your arrow keys and space bar. Sometimes people want multiple modes for viewing pictures, etc. What this enables you to do is to actually configure X Windows for multiple modes and then switch video modes while X is running using **ControlAlt+** and **ControlAlt-**. The next screen will ask you which of the selected modes you want to be your primary mode. Simply highlight the one you want to be your default mode and press Enter. Then, when you start X that will be your mode. To switch, use **ControlAlt** and + or -.

7.2.3 xf86config

`xf86config` is fairly self-documenting, with plenty of text describing its operation throughout the program. It should yield a working `/etc/XF86Config` file (which you should move to `/etc/X11/XF86Config`). It is worth noting that `xf86config` will ask you if you want it to set a link for you. This should be unnecessary on a Red Hat system.

7.3 X Window Configuration with Metro-X

By special arrangement a license to install a single copy of the Metro-X accelerated X server is included with all copies of the "Official" Red Hat

Linux CD product. Please note that unlike the XFree86 X server (also included) Metro-X is commercially licensed software. You should review and accept its license terms before installing it. Metro-X supports most of the video cards that are not supported by XFree86. The configuration utility can be run in graphical mode, (`configX`) or text mode (`configX.curses`)

7.3.1 configX.curses

`configX.curses` is a simple graphical configuration tool for configuring Metro-X. To run `configX.curses` type the command;

```
$configX.curses
```

The opening screen has information on Metro Link, Inc. and brief instructions on what you will need to configure Metro-X. Press `Enter` to begin the configuration. The configuration screen will display the current configuration information at the top and the configuration menu at the bottom. Use the arrow keys to move the highlight up and down the menu and the `Enter` key to select the highlighted item.

Graphics Card

When you select `Graphics Card` from the configuration menu a list of supported cards will be displayed. Select your video card as above. After selecting your video card you will be asked to select a video mode from a list of defaults. The resolution used is a matter of personal preference, the smaller the numbers the larger the items on the display. Some combinations of video cards and video modes will support virtual screens larger than the physical display. If your combination is one of these you will be asked to select the virtual screen size.

Mouse

Configuring your mouse with Metro-X requires that you know what type of mouse you have and how it is connected to your computer. When you select a mouse type the default device will be provided in the configuration window. If you are in doubt, accept the default and make adjustments later if needed.

Save and Exit

Selecting this from the menu will save any changes you have made to the Metro-X configuration and exit the configX.curses program.

Quit without Saving

Selecting this from the menu will discard any changes you have made to the Metro-X configuration and exit the configX.curses program.

7.3.2 configX

`configX` is a self-documented graphical version of `configX.curses`. It will start up an X server in a generic mode and allow you to configure Metro-X in a more elegant manner than `configX.curses`. In configX the `tab` key is used to move from field-to-field, the arrow keys change the value of a field, `Enter` sets/un-sets a toggle button, `Page-Up` and `Page-Down` switch between configuration pages. `ALT-F` `ALT-S` and `ALT-C` toggle the menus at the top of the page.

7.4 Sendmail

A default `sendmail.cf` file will be installed in `/etc`. The default configuration should work for most SMTP-only sites. It will *not* work for UUCP sites; you will need to generate a new `sendmail.cf` if you need to use UUCP mail transfers. To generate a new `sendmail.cf`, you will need to install `m4` and the sendmail source package. Read the `README` in the sendmail sources for more details on creating `sendmail` configuration files. Also, O'Reilly & Associates publishes a good sendmail reference entitled *sendmail* by Bryan Costales. One common sendmail configuration is to have a single machine act as a mail gateway for all the machines on your network. For instance, at Red Hat Software we have a machine `mail.redhat.com` that does all our mail. On that machine we simply need to add the names of machines for which `mail.redhat.com` will handle mail to `/etc/sendmail.cw`. Here is an example:

```
# sendmail.cw - include all aliases for your machine here.
```

```
torgo.redhat.com
poodle.redhat.com
devel.redhat.com
```

Then on the other machines, `torgo`, `poodle`, and `devel`, we need to edit `/etc/sendmail.cf` to "masquerade" as `mail.redhat.com` when sending mail, and to forward any local mail processing to `redhat.com`. Find the `DH` and `DM` lines in `/etc/sendmail.cf` and edit them thusly:

```
# who gets all local email traffic
DHredhat.com

# who I masquerade as (null for no masquerading)
DMredhat.com
```

With this type of configuration, all mail sent will appear as if it were sent from `mail.redhat.com` and any mail sent to `torgo.redhat.com` or the other hosts, will be delivered to `mail.redhat.com`.

7.5 Controlling Access to Services

As a security measure, most network services are managed by a protective program called a *TCP wrapper*. The protected services are those listed in `/etc/inetd.conf` that specify `/usr/sbin/tcpd`. `tcpd` can allow or deny access to a service based on the origin of the request, and the configuration in `/etc/hosts.allow` and `/etc/hosts.deny`. By default Red Hat Linux allows all service requests. To disable or limit services you can edit `/etc/hosts.allow`. Here is an example `/etc/hosts.allow` file:

```
ALL: redhat.com .redhat.com
in.talkd: ALL
in.ntalkd: ALL
in.fingerd: ALL
in.ftpd: ALL
```

This configuration allows all connections from `redhat.com` and `*.redhat.com` machines. It also allows talk, finger, and ftp requests from all machines.

`tcpd` allows much more sophisticated access control, using a combination of `/etc/hosts.allow` and `/etc/hosts.deny`. Read the tcpd(8) and hosts_access(5) man pages for complete details.

7.6 Anonymous FTP

Setting up anonymous FTP is simple. All you need to do is install the `anon-ftp` rpm package (which you may have already done at install time). Once it is installed, anonymous FTP will be up and running.

There are a few files you might wish to edit to configure your ftp server.

`/etc/ftpaccess` This file defines most of the access control for your ftp server. Some of the things that you can do are set up logical "groups" to control access from different sites, limit the number of simultaneous FTP connections, configure transfer logging, and much more. Read the ftpaccess man page for complete details.

`/etc/ftphosts` The ftphosts file is used to allow or deny access to certain accounts from various hosts. Read the ftphosts man page for details.

`/etc/ftpusers` This file lists all the users that are *not* allowed to ftp into your machine. For example, `root` is listed in `/etc/ftpusers` by default. That means that you can not ftp to your machine, and log in as root. This is a good security measure, but some administrators prefer to remove `root` from this file.

7.7 World Wide Web Server

If you installed the Apache web server (from the `apache` package), then your Web service is already up and running! Just point your web browser at `http://localhost`.

The default page shown is `/home/httpd/html/index.html`. You can edit this file (or completely replace it) to your liking. All the CGI programs, icons, and html pages are stored in `/home/httpd`, but this can be changed in the apache configuration files, all of which are stored in `/etc/httpd/conf`. Logs of all httpd activity are kept in `/var/log/httpd`. Setting up your web site is as easy as adding your own HTML pages and links to the `/home/httpd/html/` directory. For more information on customizing your web server there are a number of excellent books available that can help.

7.8 NFS Configuration

NFS stands for Network FileSystem, and is a way to share files between machines as if they were on your local hard drive. Linux can be both an NFS server and an NFS client, which means that it can "export" filesystems to other systems, and "mount" filesystems exported from other machines.

7.8.1 Mounting NFS Filesystems

Use the mount command to mount a NFS filesystem from another machine:

```
mount porky:/mnt/export /mnt/local
```

In the above command, `porky` is the hostname of the NFS fileserver, "/mnt/export" is the filesystem that porky is exporting, and "/mnt/local" is a directory on my local machine where I want to mount the filesystem. After the mount command runs (and if I had the proper permissions from porky) - voila! - I can 'ls /mnt/local' and get a listing of the files in /mnt/export on porky.

7.8.2 Exporting NFS Filesystems

The file that controls what filesystems you wish to export is "/etc/exports". Its format is:

```
directory        hostname(options)
```

the "(options)" are optional. For example:

```
/mnt/export      speedy.redhat.com
```

would allow `speedy.redhat.com` to mount /mnt/export, but:

```
/mnt/export     speedy.redhat.com(ro)
```

would only allow speedy to mount /mnt/export read-only.

Each time you change /etc/exports, you need to tell the NFS daemons to examine it for new information. One simple way to accomplish this is to just stop and start the daemons:

```
/etc/rc.d/init.d/nfs stop
/etc/rc.d/init.d/nfs start
```

The following will also work:

```
killall -HUP rpc.nfsd rpc.mountd
```

7.8.3 Further Reading

See the following man pages for more details: nfsd(8), mountd(8), and exports(5). Another good reference is "Managing NFS and NIS Services" published by O'Reilly & Associates.

7.9 Rebuilding the Kernel

The best source of documentation on rebuilding your kernel should already be installed on your system. If you installed the `ldp` package, you should be able to `cd` to `/usr/doc/HOWTO` where you'll find many howto documents including the Kernel-HOWTO. They may be gzipped, so you may need to `zcat Kernel-HOWTO | more` to see its contents.

7.10 Running Programs at Boot Time

The file `/etc/rc.d/rc.local` is executed at boot time, after all other initialization is complete. You can add additional initialization commands here. For instance, you may want to start up additional daemons, or initialize a printer or something. In addition, if you require serial port setup, you can edit `/etc/rc.d/rc.serial` and it will get executed automatically at boot time.

The default `/etc/rc.d/rc.local` simply creates a nice login banner with your kernel version and machine type.

7.11 UUCP Setup

The text of this section was contributed by Julien Michielsen and others. For those of you who would like to setup uucp, these configuration files might be useful to you. This documentation covers the use of UUCP with `smail` instead of `sendmail`. Red Hat ships with sendmail configured, but you can uninstall it (`rpm -u sendmail`) and install the `smail` RPM from the contrib directory on your CD or `ftp.redhat.com`.

7.11.1 The Basics

This is a leaf-site in the `hobby.nl` domain. The provider is `hgatenl.hobby.nl`. A local second provider (`murphy.hobby.nl`) can also be called. He is a forwarder for news.

Things to do:

- make sure `/dev/modem` exists. If not, make a symbolic link between modem and the cua?-port your modem is on (cua0=com1, cua1=com2, ...).
- permissions of `/dev/cua3` are `crw-rw-rw-`
- create the file `/var/log/uucp`, ownership `uucp.uucp`, permissions `-rw-rw-r--`
- create the directory `/etc/uucp`, and create the files `dial`, `port` and `sys` in there. Ownership `/etc/uucp` is `uucp.uucp`. (Also of the files in /etc/uucp.)

7.11.2 Sample Configuration Files

`/etc/uucp/sys`:

```
remote-send ~
remote-receive ~
local-send ~
local-receive ~
command-path /usr/sbin
commands rmail
#time Wk1800-0700,Sa,Su
time any
port ACU
max-remote-debug none
#debug chat

#protocol-parameter i

system murphy
commands rmail
call-login Ukennis
#          ^ may be specific for this situation
call-password NotKnown
phone 0109876543

system hgatenl
commands rmail
call-password MySecret
chat "" \d\d\d ogin: \dSkennis sword: Secret "" \d\d Uucp u
phone 0206781234
```

/etc/uucp/dial:

```
dialer hayesnormal
chat "" ATZ\r\c\d\d OK\r ATQ0M1E0\r\c OK\r AT\&K1\r\c OK\r ATDT\T\r\c CONNECT
chat-fail RING\r
chat-fail NO\sCARRIER
chat-fail ERROR
chat-fail NO\sDIALTONE
chat-fail BUSY
chat-fail NO\sANSWER
chat-fail VOICE
complete \d\d+++\d\dATH\r\c
abort \d\d+++\d\dATH\r\c
```

/etc/uucp/port:

```
port ACU
type modem
baud 38400
device /dev/modem
carrier true
dialer hayesnormal
```

7.11.3 Smail Configuration

Subsequently install the smail RPM. Use the `smail.3.1.29.i386.rpm`, it works fine. In the `/etc/smail` directory make an entry in this form: `/etc/smail/config` :

```
hostname=kennis.hobby.nl
domains=hobby.nl
smart_path=hgatenl
# max_message_size=512k
# domains=foo.bar

# smart_path=isp
# uucp_name=hname.foo.bar
# visible_name=foo.bar
# auth_domains=foo.bar
# more_hostnames=nonfoo:nonfoo.foo.bar
```

Create `/etc/smail/maps/map`:

```
#N      foo.bar foo2.bar2
#S      AT 486/RedHat Linux 1.2.13
#O      organization
#C      contact
#E      administration (email)
#T      phone
#P      address
#R
#U      hosts connected via uucp
#W      created/edited by
#
# hname isp
```

```
# hname foo.bar

# hname = foo.bar
# hname = hname.foo.bar
kennis  .hobby.nl(LOCAL)
kennis = kennis.hobby.nl
hgatenl kennis(DIRECT)
```

7.12 Color ls Setup

Some Linux distributions include, by default, an ls program that uses colors to indicate directories, executables, etc. Red Hat Linux does not ship this way, but it is easy to set up. This section describes the simple steps you need to take to use color ls.

7.12.1 Installing the color-ls RPM

First, check to see if you have color-ls installed:

```
rpm -q color-ls
```

If rpm reports that color-ls is not installed, you'll need to install it from your CD-ROM in the `RedHat/RPMS` directory, or download it from `ftp://ftp.redhat.com`. Install it with:

```
rpm -ivh color-ls-3.12.0.3-2.i386.rpm
```

(or with whatever the name of the rpm file is).

7.12.2 Initializing Color ls

At your shell prompt (this should work for bash and csh/tcsh):

```
eval `dircolors`
```

(Use backquotes around dircolors, not forward quotes.)

From then on, if you are on the console, using rxvt or using xterm-color, when you type 'ls' your listing will be in color according to file type.

7.12.3 Making Color ls the Default

Making color-ls the default for you or your machine is easy. If you just want color-ls to be the default for you, put:

```
eval 'dircolors'
```

(Use backquotes around dircolors, not forward quotes.)

in your $HOME/.bashrc if you use bash and your $HOME/.cshrc if you use csh/tcsh.

If you want color-ls to be the default for everyone on your machine, put:

```
eval 'dircolors'
```

(Use backquotes around dircolors, not forward quotes.)

in your `/etc/bashrc` for bash and `/etc/csh.cshrc` for csh/tcsh.

7.12.4 Further Reading

For complete details, read the color-ls and dircolors man pages.

7.13 NIS/NYS Setup

The basic content of this section was donated by Grant Taylor. It was edited for clarity and space. Other content was contributed by users on the redhat-list mailing list.

7.13.1 How do I use the NYS/NIS system that comes with Red Hat?

This text attempts to describe the yp, NIS, and NIS+ support offered in the Red Hat 2.x Linux products.

- What is yp? NIS? NIS+? NYS? These questions are answered in the NIS-HOWTO. Read it - it even comes with Red Hat in the ldp RPM and on the CD-ROM. If you install the ldp RPM, you will find the NIS-HOWTO in `/usr/doc/HOWTO`.

  The quick answer is that while yp ("Yellow Pages") is the phone book in Britain, NIS is the traditional RPC-based implementation for sharing passwd, group, hosts, services, and other useful things between many machines. NIS+ is a snazzier, and more secure reimplementation of the same idea. NYS is the public domain version of same.

- What *is* offered? Red Hat ships NYS client code in its libc and plain yp/NIS client programs like ypcat and ypbind. We ship a plain NIS server daemon, since the NYS (aka NIS+) server daemon is not yet ready for prime-time. Our ypserv does not appear to have the tcp_wrapper-style /etc/hosts.allow/deny checking compiled in.

- How the heck do I get ypbind to work properly? How do I set up a client workstation? The NYS code in libc does it all. There is no need to run ypbind. You probably DO need to run domainname (apparently for the benefit of of plain NIS client programs). You must configure which maps are read from where in /etc/nsswitch.conf, and which NIS server and domain you are in using /etc/yp.conf. nsswitch.conf has comments galore, and yp.conf will look like this:

  ```
  domain foo
  ypserver foo.bar.com
  ```

  Do not put the usual +:::: lines at the end of passwd or group.

  Netgroups are not supported under RH ¡=2.1; adding netwroup entries (like +@foo or -@foo) to passwd or group can compromise the security of your system. NYS netgroups do work in libc ¿= 5.2.?; Future Red Hat releases will probably use such a libc.

- ypcat and ypmatch don't work! In 2.0 and 2.1, the ypcat and ypmatch binaries don't work. You should be able to compile working versions from the NYS source in libc-5.0.9. If you are unable to do this, please email support@redhat.com asking for an updated package.

- How do I run ypserv (master)? Red Hat ships a plain NIS (aka yp) server. It works just like any other ypserv - modify the makefile in /var/nis to taste, perhaps move the source files into `/var/nis/src`, or perhaps not, run a make to make the databases, and run ypserv. Further documentation is in `/usr/doc/ypserv*/*`.

- Where's yppasswd and yppasswdd? We don't ship it, but you can obtain the regular distribution and install it yourself without too much hassle. It is available from the places listed in the NIS HOWTO. You have to modify the pwupdate script that comes with it, even though the README claims it works with the NYS Makefile we ship. We also don't ship a `rpcsrv/yppasswd.h`, although we do have the `.x` file. The yppasswdd package comes with both so it doesn't matter much. The NYS define should be used, but don't use the -lnsl library since it is built into our libc.

- This information is miserably incomplete! There is already an NIS-HOWTO that describes how to set things up far better than this document does or should. Read it - it comes with Red Hat in the ldp package.

7.14 INN Setup

7.14.1 Getting Started

First and foremost, here is some recommended reading:

- INND FAQ (found on the redhat CDROM, and should be installed in `/usr/doc/inn-1.4unoff3-2`
- README.RHCL (found in the same directory)
- Unix System Administration Handbook, by Nemeth, ie. "the red book"
- news.software.nntp Usenet newsgroup. Full of newbie and esoteric questions. You aren't as dumb as you think you are.

For starters. We'll assume you just installed your RHL distribution, and now want to run INN. If you started INN as root, you have totally screwed up the permissions for all the files. You should probably uninstall and re-install the INN package. DO NOT run the INN BINARIES AS ROOT!! This is a common error. When editing, copying and renaming files, do so as the `news` user. The easiest way to do this is to log in as root and type the command `su news`.

7.14.2 Disk Space Requirements

Disk space and memory issues: You need around 2 GB of space to run a small feed, and probably at least 4 GB to run a full feed. The Nemeth book says you need 64 MB of ram, but 40 MB should be ok for a small user base. If you can, devote the entire machine to INN, as it is a memory and CPU pig.

Now for the configuration. Let's make some assumptions: Your feed site is `news.redhat.com`, and your site is `news.rookie.com`. Since news is most likely an alias for another host name, lets say `news.redhat.com` is `blue.redhat.com` and `news.rookie.com` is `green.rookie.com` Now you need to edit the control files.

active

You need to obtain a copy of an active file. This is the list of newsgroups that you will carry on your system. If you want a full feed, get the active file from your feed site, and edit it at will. However, before you use the active file from another site, it will need to be modified. Copy the active file to `/var/lib/news` (this is where your history file, active file, active.times and newsgroups file go). There will probably be a placeholder active file there, and you may safely delete it, since it isn't what you want to use. Rename your acquired active file to "upstream.active" and process it with the following command:

```
cat upstream.active | awk '{ printf(%s 000000000 000000000 %s\n, $1, $4)
}' > active
```

(This should all be on one line.)

You should now have an active file with all 000000000's in it.

newsgroups

You now need to obtain your upstream `newsgroups` file, which contains descriptions of the active newsgroups. This file also should exist in the `/var/lib/news` subdirectory. You should now be done with the `/var/lib/news` subdirectory.

expire.ctl

You should now go to the `/etc/news` subdirectory. You want to edit the `expire.ctl` file, which is used by the expire program. An initial `expire.ctl` file may look like this:

```
/remember/:14

*:A:3:4:5
```

newsfeeds

You now need to edit the `newsfeeds` file. This file indicates how articles should be sent to upstream or downstream sites. The newsfeed file is sensitive to typos, so be careful. You need an entry in the newsfeeds file pointing at your feeder site. You need this in your newsfeeds file:

```
ME\

:*,!control,!junk,!rookie.*::\

redhat.com\

:*,!control,!junk\

:Tf,Wnm:news.redhat.com
```

These two entries should be near the top of your newsfeeds file.

nnrp.access

The `nnrp.access` file allows newsreader clients access to the news server. To allow hosts in the rookie.com domain to read news, this entry should be in `nnrp.access`:

```
*.rookie.com:Read Post:::*
```

hosts.nntp

This file tells INN which hosts are allow to transfer articles to the local site. Any hosts not listed in this file are handed off to the `nnrp.access` file. Important, you need to have your local hostname listed in this file!

news.rookie.com should have this in its `hosts.nntp` file:

```
news.redhat.com

blue.redhat.com

green.rookie.com
```

You may not need to place the actual hostname in there, but it won't hurt. Remember, in the above example, news and blue are both hostnames for the same machine in the redhat.com domain.

inn.conf

```
organization: Top Server

server: green.rookie.com

domain: rookie.com

fromhost: green.rookie.com
```

```
moderatormailer: %s@uunet.uu.net

pathhost: green.rookie.com
```

innwatch.ctl

In the last line of this command, there is a `print $3`. This should be changed to `print $4`.

nntpsend.ctl

This file needs to be edited.

```
redhat.com:blue.redhat.com::
```

passwd.nntp

```
blue.redhat.com::

news.redhat.com::
```

Other tasks:

We are just about there. We now need to make sure the `news.daily` script gets run once a day in order to be articles get expired and such. This entry needs to be added to news's chrontab:

```
6 4 * * * /usr/lib/news/bin/news.daily > /dev/null 2>&1 &
```

Edit `/etc/rc.d/rc.news` and change `DOINNWATCH=false` to `DOINNWATCH=true`

Ok, you should now be able to reboot, and INN should be running when you come back up. Assuming your feed is `turned on/`, you should start getting articles. Examine the `/var/log/messages` file to see how things are going. Since the user `news` will send messages to itself, you will want to edit the `/etc/aliases` file so that messages sent to news get sent to your user account.

7.14.3 What to do if things don't work...

- Check permissions. Go to `/usr/lib/news/bin`, and `su` to news. Run `inncheck -perms` and check to see if any permissions need to be changed. DO NOT change the permission for inndstart though-that will keep INND from loading. If you do change any permissions, be sure to record each change you make, so you can go back and change them earlier. If you get messages like this: `ME: can't open file`, make sure the news user has read or write access to that file. As far as I know, all of the configuration files need to be owned by news, and exist in the news group.

- Make sure your feed is sending.

- Look through the FAQ's. Lots of questions are answered in there. I hope this primer has been useful. As far as I know, this text only applies to the default INN distribution that comes with Red Hat Linux 2.1, and may not be pertinant to any other Linux distributions. If you see any errors or omissions, feel free to point them out.

Chapter 8

Finding Documentation

Red Hat includes thousands of pages of online documentation to help you learn how to use the system. The man pages, info documents, and plain text files it includes provide information on almost every aspect of Linux. For more help, Red Hat also includes all of the documentation produced by the Linux Documentation Project electronically.

8.1 On Line Help

When you are looking for general help on commands and error messages, the best place to start is right on your system.

8.1.1 Man Pages

Most every command on your system has an associated "man" page. This is documentation that you can get to instantly should you have questions or problems. If you were having trouble with the command `ls`, you could enter `man ls`. This will bring up the man page for `ls`. The man page is viewed through the `less` program, so all of the options to `less` will work while in a man page. Some important key strokes are:

- `q` to quit

- `Enter` to page down line by line
- `Space` to page down page by page
- `b` to page back up by one page
- `/` followed by a string and `Enter` to search for a string
- `n` to find the next occurance of the previous search

Sometimes viewing man pages isn't too friendly on line. Providing you have a working printer, you can print man pages as well. If you don't have postscript printing capability and just want to print ASCII, you can print man pages with:

```
man COMMAND | groff -mandoc -Tascii | lpr
```

If you do have a postscript printer, you will probably want to print with:

```
man COMMAND | groff -mandoc | lpr
```

In both of those commands substitute "COMMAND" for the command you are trying to get help for.

Also, sometimes things have more than one man page. Here is a table of what is located where:

```
Section    Contents
-------    ----------------
   1       user commands
   2       system calls
   3       library calls
   4       devices
   5       file formats
   6       games
   7       miscellaneous
   8       system commands
   9       kernel internals
```

So, let's say that you want to see the man page for `swapon`. You do `man swapon`. You will actually get the man page for the system call `swapon(2)`, which is the function you use in a C program to turn swap on. Unless you are writing your own program to do it, this probably isn't what you want. So, using the chart above, you can see that what you want is probably a "system command" and is located in section 8. You can then do `man 8 swapon`. All of this is because `man` searches the man directories in order, and then returns when it finds the first match.

You can also search the man pages for strings. You do this using `man -k string_to_search_for`. This won't work, however, unless the database is created. Under Red Hat, this gets done by a cron job overnight. If you don't leave your system on overnight you won't have the database. If that is the case, just run:

```
/usr/sbin/makewhatis /usr/man /usr/X11R6/man
```

Note: This must be done as root. Once you've done that, you could do `man -k swapon`. That would return:

```
# man -k swapon
swapon, swapoff (2)   - start/stop swapping to file/device
swapon, swapoff (8)   - enable/disable devices and files for paging and swapping
swapon, swapoff (2)   - start/stop swapping to file/device
swapon, swapoff (8)   - enable/disable devices and files for paging and swapping
```

So you can see that there are pages in section 2 and 8 both referring to swapon (and swapoff in this case).

8.1.2 Package Documentation

Many packages of software have READMEs and other documentation as part of the source package. We have come up with a standard place to install those documents for you so that you don't have to install the sources to look at the documents. All of those documents are stored in subdirectories of `/usr/doc`. The subdirectory depends on the package. Each package that has extra documentation will create a directory called packagename-version-releasenumber. For example, the tin package might be version 1.22 and release number 2. The path to its documentation would be `/usr/doc/tin-1.22-2`.

For the most part, the documents in this directory are ASCII. You can usually view them with `more filename` or `less filename`. This is nice, but what if you want to see if there is documentation for a specific command or file and you don't know the package it came from? It doesn't matter! You can simply do:

```
rpm -qdf /etc/sendmail.cf
```

This will report all the documentation from the package containing the file `/etc/sendmail.cf`. Commands like this are covered more in depth in the RPM-HOWTO, most likely available wherever you got this document.

Also, what if it's a command you need help with and the man page isn't good? You could do something like:

```
rpm -qdf 'which COMMAND'
```

Again, where "COMMAND" is the actual command you need help with. This will only work when the command is on your path.

8.1.3 HOWTOs and FAQs

Most of the contents of the Linux Documentation Project (LDP) are available in `/usr/doc` on your system.

`/usr/doc/HOWTO` contains the ASCII versions of all the available HOWTOs at the time we pressed the CD-ROM. They are gzipped, so you will have to use `gunzip` to unzip them or you will have to use something like:

```
zcat HAM-HOWTO.gz {\verbar} more
```

The latter will work, but is a bit less flexible than unzipping and then using `more`. It also requires more disk space unless you re-gzip the document when done.

`/usr/doc/HOWTO/mini` contains the ASCII versions of all the available mini-HOWTOs. They are not compressed and can be viewed with `more` or `less`. `/usr/doc/HTML` contains the HTML versions of all the HOWTOs and the _Linux Installation and Getting Started_ guide. To view things here, just use a WWW browser like `Arena` (included in the Red Hat distribution). You would do something like:

```
cd /usr/doc/HTML
arena index.html
```

`/usr/doc/FAQ` contains ASCII version (and some HTML versions) of some popular FAQs, including the RedHat-FAQ. All of them can be viewed using `more` or `less`.

8.1.4 The "locate" Command

When you don't know the full name of a command or file, but need to find it, you can usually find it with `locate`. `locate` uses a database to find all files on your system. Normally, this database gets built from a cron job every night. This won't happen, however, if your machine isn't booted into Linux all the time. So, if that is the case, you may occasionally want to run the following command:

```
/usr/bin/updatedb --prunepaths='/tmp /proc /mnt /var/tmp /dev'
```

You will need to be root on your system when doing that. That will allow `locate` to work properly.

So, if you know you need to find all the "finger" files, you could run:

```
locate finger
```

It should return something like:

```
/usr/bin/finger
/usr/lib/irc/script/finger
/usr/man/man1/finger.1
/usr/man/man8/in.fingerd.8
/usr/sbin/in.fingerd
```

One thing to note, however, is that `locate` not only returns hits based on file name, but also on path name. So if you have a `/home/djb/finger/` directory on your system, it would get returned along with all files in the directory.

8.1.5 "info" Pages

While `man` is the most ubiquitous documentation format, `info` is much more powerful. It provides hypertext links to make reading large documents much easier and many features for the documentation writer. There are some very complete `info` documents on various aspects of Red Hat (especially the portions from the GNU project).

To read `info` documentation, use the `info` program without any arguments. It will present you with a list of available documentation. If it can't find something, it's probably because you don't have the package installed that includes that documentation. Install it with RPM and try again.

If you're comfortable using emacs, it has a built in browser for `info` documentation. Use `C-h C-i` to see it.

The `info` system is a hypertext based system. Any highlighted text that appears is a link leading to more information. Use the `Tab` key to move the cursor to the link, and press `Enter` to follow the link. Pressing `p` returns you to the previous page, `n` moves you to the next page, and `u` goes up one level of documentation. To exit `info`, press `C-x C-c` (that's control-x followed by control-c).

The best way to learn how to use `info` is to read the info documentation on it. If you read the first screen that `info` presents you'll be able to get started.

8.2 Help from the Internet Community

8.2.1 Red Hat Mailing Lists

If you can't find help for your problem on line and you have WWW access, you should see http://www.redhat.com/mailing-list.html. Here you can search the archives of the redhat-list. Most all questions have already been answered there.

If you've exhausted all options in finding help for your problem, you next best alternative is to ask for help on the Red Hat Mailing Lists. For the most up to date info, see http://www.redhat.com/mailing-list.html.

The request addresses for each of our lists is:

```
redhat-list-request@redhat.com
redhat-digest-request@redhat.com
redhat-announce-list-request@redhat.com
redhat-devel-list-request@redhat.com
rpm-list-request@redhat.com
axp-list-request@redhat.com
sparc-list-request@redhat.com
```

To subscribe, send mail to the address of the list you want to subscribe to with "subscribe" in the Subject line.

To unsubscribe, send mail to the address of the list you want to unsubscribe from with "unsubscribe" in the Subject line.

Then to send mail to the list, you just send it to the address above without the "-request" in the name. The only exception to this is the redhat-digest which is only a digest version the redhat-list. In that case the address is "redhat-list@redhat.com".

8.2.2 USENET Newsgroups

Another good source of help is the comp.os.linux hierarchy on USENET. If you are familiar with news, you should check it out. There will be a "Using News" Tips document in the future to assist those unfamiliar with Usenet.

Chapter 9

Package Management with RPM

9.1 Introduction

RPM is the **R**ed Hat **P**ackage **M**anager. While it does contain Red Hat in the name, it is completely intended to be an open packaging system available for anyone to use. It allows users to take source code for new software and package it into source and binary form such that binaries can be easily installed and tracked and source can be rebuilt easily. It also maintains a database of all packages and their files that can be used for verifying packages and querying for information about files and/or packages.

Red Hat Software encourages other distribution vendors to take the time to look at RPM and use it for their own distributions. RPM is quite flexible and easy to use, though it provides the base for a very extensive system. It is also completely open and available, though we would appreciate bug reports and fixes. Permission is granted to use and distribute RPM royalty free under the GPL.

RPM can even provide an excellent method to upgrade an existing system. The database won't be as up to date as a machine that was completely installed with RPM, but it will still contain anything installed with RPM. It can also be used to package commercial software.

9.2 Overview

First, let me state some of the philosophy behind RPM. One design goal was to allow the use of "pristine" sources. With RPP (our former packaging system from which *none* of RPM is derived), our source packages were the "hacked" sources that we built from. Theoretically, one could install a source RPP and then `make` it with no problems. But the sources were not the original ones, and there was no reference as to what changes we had to make to get it to build. One had to download the pristine sources separately. With RPM, you have the pristine sources along with a patch that we used to compile from. We see this as a big advantage. Why? Several reasons. For one, if a new version of a program comes out, you don't necessarily have to start from scratch to get it to compile under RHL. You can look at the patch to see what you *might* need to do. All the compile-in defaults are easily visible this way.

RPM is also designed to have powerful querying options. You can do searches through your entire database for packages or just certain files. You can also easily find out what package a file belongs to and where it came from. The RPM files themselves are compressed archives, but you can query individual packages easily and *quickly* because of a custom binary header added to the package with everything you could possibly need to know contained in uncompressed form. This allows for *fast* querying.

Another powerful feature is the ability to verify packages. If you are worried that you deleted an important file for some package, just verify it. You will be notified of any anomalies. At that point, you can reinstall the package if necessary. Any config files that you had are preserved as well.

We would like to thank the folks from the BOGUS distribution for many of their ideas and concepts that are included in RPM. While RPM was completely written by Red Hat Software, its operation is based on code written by the BOGUS team (PM and PMS).

9.3 General Information

9.3.1 Acquiring RPM

The best way to get RPM is to install Red Hat Linux. If you don't want to do that, you can still get and use RPM. It can be acquired from any Official Red Hat Mirror. Some of those are:

```
FTP Site                   Directory
========                   =========
ftp.cms.uncwil.edu         /linux/redhat
ftp.wilmington.net         /linux/redhat
ftp.pht.com                /pub/linux/redhat
sunsite.unc.edu            /pub/Linux/distributions/redhat
sunsite.doc.ic.ac.uk       /packages/linux/sunsite.unc-mirror/
                                   distributions/redhat/
ftp.caldera.com            /pub/mirrors/redhat
ftp.lasermoon.co.uk        /pub/distributions/RedHat
ftp.cc.gatech.edu          /pub/linux/distributions/redhat
uiarchive.cso.uiuc.edu     /pub/systems/linux/distributions/redhat
ftp.ibp.fr                 /pub/linux/distributions/redhat
ftp.gwdg.de                /pub/linux/install/redhat
ftp.uoknor.edu             /linux/redhat
ftp.msu.ru                 /pub/Linux/RedHat
linux.ucs.indiana.edu      /pub/linux/redhat
ftp.cvut.cz                /pub/linux/redhat
ftp.ton.tut.fi             /pub/Linux/RedHat
ftp.funet.fi               /pub/Linux/images/RedHat
```

We are unsure at this point where to find it past there, but it will most likely just be a directory called RPM. We will make a tar file available with a README containing all the install instructions you should need.

9.3.2 RPM Requirements

The main requirement to run RPM is Perl 5.x. All of RPM is written in Perl. You must also have a working copy of `cpio` and `gunzip`, which most Linux distributions have now. While this system is intended for use with Linux, it may very well be portable to other Unix systems who meet the above conditions. Be warned, the binary packages generated on a different type of Unix system will not be compatible.

Those are the minimal requirements to install RPMs. To build RPMs from source, you also need everything normally required to build a package, like `gcc`, `make`, etc.

9.4 Using RPM

In its simplest form, RPM can be used to install packages:

```
rpm -i foobar-1.0-1.i386.rpm
```

The next simplest command is to uninstall a package:

```
rpm -u foobar
```

One of the more complex but *highly* useful commands allows you to install packages via FTP. If you are connected to the net and want to install a new package, all you need to do is specify the file with a valid URL, like so:

```
rpm -i ftp://ftp.pht.com/pub/RPMS/foobar-1.0-1.i386.rpm
```

Please note, however, that the current version of RPM will only do installs via FTP. You cannot run any of the more complex query options on packages at an FTP site.

While these are simple commands, rpm can be used in a multitude of ways as seen from the `Usage` message. To see the `Usage` message, just type `rpm` and hit Enter.

First, I'll go through a synopsis of what all the options mean (don't worry, there may be alot of options, but we tried to make them all as intuitive as possible).

Options are nested, so the possible options are many. Here's a description in parallel with the `Usage` message:

- `help` prints the usage message
- `-i` installs an rpm file.

  - `--hash, -h` is a very cool option for watching the package install (much like 'hash' in ftp).
  - `--percent` prints the percentages as a package installs (but is only useful for interfacing with other tools...is not really human readable).
  - `--force` will force an install of a binary package even though it may already exist in the database.
  - `--test` will tell you if installing would work or not (do you have a conflict with an already installed package).
  - `--root` will install a package using the root prefix specified instead of using the default of `/`.

- `--install` installs an rpm file.
- `-U` upgrades a package. This option installs the new package and then uninstalls the old one without hurting the new one. The upgrade option takes the same options as the install option.
- `-q` is the query option. In its simplest form, you can do `rpm -q foobar` which would return `foobar-1.0-1`. (1.0 is the version number, 1 is the release number.)
- Several options may be used with `-q`:
  - `-a` will query all currently installed packages.
  - `-f <file>` will query the package owning <file>.
  - `-F` is the same as `-f` except you can give it filenames via stdin (ie. `ls /usr/bin | rpm -qF`).
  - `-p <packagefile>` will query the package. It is really only useful when combined with one of the Information Selection Options below.
  - `-P` is like -p, except it takes its package filenames from stdin (ie. `ls /mnt/redhat/redhat-3.0/RPMS | rpm -qP`).
  - `--root` will query a mounted filesystem.
- Several Information Selection Options can be used with any combination of the above options. If none is given, the package name only is displayed.
  - `-i` displays package information such as Name, Description, Release, etc.

  - `-l` will display the file list from the entire package (all files that get installed). You can also use a `-v` with this to make the file list much more verbose.
  - `-s` shows you the state of all the files in the package. There are only two possible states, normal and missing.
  - `-d` outputs a list of just the files marked as documentation (man pages, info pages, READMEs, etc). `-v` will give even more info.
  - `-c` outputs a list of only the configuration files (sendmail.cf, passwd, inittab, etc.) `-v` will give more info about the files.

- {`-V`,`-y`,`--verify`} are the verify options. All are interchangeable. They all take the same Package Specification and Information Selection options as the `-q` option. I'll list some examples:
  - To verify a package containing particular file, do:

    ```
    rpm -yf /bin/vi
    ```

  - To verify ALL your files, do:

    ```
    rpm -ya
    ```

  - To verify files on your system versus the files in a .rpm file, do:

    ```
    rpm -Vp foobar-1.0-1.rpm
    ```

- `--uninstall, -u` <package> to uninstall a package
- `-b` to build a package (from sources and a spec file). This option will be discussed more at length in the next section, Building RPMs.
- `-v` be verbose in the output of what's going on.
- `-vv` be *very* verbose in the output of what's going on.

9.5 Now what can I *really* do with RPM?

RPM is a very useful tool and, as you can see, has several options. The best way to make sense of them is to look at some examples. I covered simple install/uninstall above, so here are some more examples:

- Let's say you delete some files by accident, but you aren't sure what you deleted. If you want to verify your entire system and see what might be missing, you would do:

```
rpm -Va
```

- Let's say you run across a file that you don't recognize. To find out which package owns it, you would do:

  ```
  rpm -qf /usr/X11R6/bin/xjewel
  ```

  The output would be:

  ```
  xjewel-1.6-1
  ```

- You find a new koules RPM, but you don't know what it is. To find out some information on it, do:

  ```
  rpm -qpi koules-1.0-1.i386.rpm
  ```

  The output would be:

  ```
  Name         : koules       Distribution: RHL 2.1
  Version      : 1.0          Vendor: Red Hat Software
  Release      : 1            Build date: Tue Aug 29
  Install date: never         Build host: daffy.redhat.com
  Group        : Games
  Size         : 403105
  Description : SVGAlib game
  ```

- Now you want to see what files the koules RPM installs. You would do:

  ```
  rpm -qpl koules-1.0-1.i386.rpm
  ```

  The output is:

  ```
  /usr/man/man6/koules.6
  /usr/lib/games/kouleslib/start.raw
  /usr/lib/games/kouleslib/end.raw
  /usr/lib/games/kouleslib/destroy2.raw
  /usr/lib/games/kouleslib/destroy1.raw
  /usr/lib/games/kouleslib/creator2.raw
  /usr/lib/games/kouleslib/creator1.raw
  /usr/lib/games/kouleslib/colize.raw
  /usr/lib/games/kouleslib
  /usr/games/koules
  ```

These are just several examples. More creative ones can be thought of really easy once you are familiar with RPM.

9.6 Building RPMs

Building RPMs is fairly easy to do, especially if you can get the software you are trying to package to build on its own.

The basic procedure to build an RPM is as follows:

- Make sure your `/etc/rpmrc` is setup for your system.
- Get the source code you are building the RPM for to build on your system.
- Make a patch of any changes you had to make to the sources to get them to build properly.
- Make a spec file for the package.
- Make sure everything is in its proper place.
- Build the package using RPM.

Under normal operation, RPM builds both binary and source packages.

9.6.1 The rpmrc File

Right now, the only configuration of RPM is available via the `/etc/rpmrc` file. An example one looks like:

```
require_vendor: 1
require_distribution: 1
require_group: 1
distribution: RHL 2.1
vendor: Red Hat Software
arch_sensitive: 1
topdir: /usr/src/redhat

optflags: i386 -O2 -m486
optflags: axp -O2
```

The `require_vendor` line causes RPM to require that it find a vendor line. This can come from the `/etc/rpmrc` or from the header of the spec file itself. To turn this off, change the number to `0`. The same holds true for the `require_distribution` and `require_group` lines.

The next line is the `distribution` line. You can define that here or later in the header of the spec file. When building for a particular distribution, it's a good idea to make sure this line is correct, even though it is not required. The `vendor` line works much the same way, but can be anything (ie. Joe's Software and Rock Music Emporium).

The next line is `arch_sensitive`. This specifies where the binary RPMs go and what they are named. Right now, i386 is defined as a type within RPM. That means if you are building on an Intel machine and have this value set to true, your RPMs will go in `/usr/src/redhat/RPMS/i386/` and their name will be something like `foobar-1.0-1.i386.rpm`. If you set this value to `0`, the RPMs will be placed in `/usr/src/redhat/RPMS/` and will be named something like `foobar-1.0-1.bin.rpm`. This does not affect the name or placement of the source RPM, however.

RPM also now has support for building packages on multiple architectures. The `rpmrc` file can hold an "optflags" variable for building things that require architecture specific flags when building. See later sections for how to use this variable.

In addition to the above macros, there are several more. You can use:

- `topdir` to specify the top level directory for building. In Red Hat the default top level directory is `/usr/src/redhat`.
- `specdir` is the directory under topdir to use for the spec files. The default for this is `SPECS`.
- `builddir` specifies the top level of the build directory. The default for this is `BUILD`.
- `sourcedir` specifies the top level of the source directory. The default for this is `SOURCES`. This is where the pristine tar files, the patches, and the icons go.
- `rpmdir` sets the directory for the binary RPMs. The default for this is `RPMS`.
- `srcrpmdir` sets the directory for the source RPMs. The default for this is `SRPMS`.

- `docdir` specifies where the documentation should be installed. By default, this is `/usr/doc`.
- `libdir` sets the path for the RPM database. By default, this is `/var/lib/rpm`.
- `timecheck` sets whether or not to do a timecheck by default.

9.6.2 The Spec File

We'll begin with discussion of the spec file. Spec files are required to build a package. The spec file is a description of the software along with instructions on how to build it and a file list for all the binaries that get installed.

You'll want to name your spec file according to a standard convention. It should be the package name-dash-version number-dash-release number-dot-spec.

Here is a small spec file (vim-3.0-1.spec):

```
Description: VIsual editor iMproved
Name: vim
Version: 3.0
Release: 1
Icon: vim.gif
Source: sunsite.unc.edu:/pub/Linux/apps/editors/vi/vim-3.0.tar.gz
Patch: vim-3.0-make.patch
Copyright: distributable
Group: Applications/Editors

%prep
%setup
%patch -p1
cd src
cp makefile.unix makefile

%build
cd src
make

%install
rm -f /bin/vim
```

```
cd src
make install
ln -sf vim /bin/vi

%files
%doc doc/reference.doc doc/unix.doc tutor/tutor
/bin/vim
/bin/vi
/usr/man/man1/vim.1
/usr/lib/vim.hlp
```

9.6.3 The Header

The header has some standard fields in it that you need to fill in. There are a few caveats as well. The fields must be filled in as follows:

- `Description:` This one is kind of obvious. You can span multiple lines by ending each line with a backslash.
- `Name:` This must be the name string from the rpm filename you plan to use.
- `Version:` This must be the version string from the rpm filename you plan to use.
- `Release:` This is the release number for a package of the same version (ie. if we make a package and find it to be slightly broken and need to make it again, the next package would be release number 2).
- `Icon:` This is the name of the icon file for use by other high level installation tools (like Red Hat's "glint"). It must be a gif and resides in the SOURCES directory.
- `Source:` This line points at the HOME location of the pristine source file. It is used if you ever want to get the source again or check for newer versions. Caveat: The filename in this line MUST match the filename you have on your own system (ie. don't download the source file and change its name). You can also specify more than one source file using lines like:

  ```
  Source0: blah-0.tar.gz
  Source1: blah-1.tar.gz
  Source2: fooblah.tar.gz
  ```

These files would go in the `SOURCES` directory. (The directory structure is discussed in a later section, "The Source Directory Tree".)

- `Patch:` This is the place you can find the patch if you need to download it again. Caveat: The filename here must match the one you use when you make YOUR patch. You may also want to note that you can have multiple patch files much as you can have multiple sources.] You would have something like:

```
Patch0: blah-0.patch
Patch1: blah-1.patch
Patch2: fooblah.patch
```

  These files would go in the `SOURCES` directory.

- `Copyright:` This line tells how a package is copyrighted. You should use something like GPL, BSD, MIT, public domain, distributable, or commercial.

- `Root:` This line allows you to specify a directory as the "root" for building and installing the new package. You can use this to help test your package before having it installed on your machine.

- `Group:` This line is used to tell high level installation programs (such as Red Hat's "glint") where to place this particular program in its hierarchical structure. The group tree currently looks something like this:

```
Applications
    Communications
    Editors
        Emacs
    Engineering
    Spreadsheets
    Databases
    Graphics
    Networking
    Mail
    Math
    News
    Publishing
        TeX
Base
    Kernel
Utilities
```

```
        Archiving
        Console
        File
        System
        Terminal
        Text
    Daemons
    Documentation
    X11
        XFree86
            Servers
        Applications
            Graphics
            Networking
        Games
            Strategy
            Video
        Amusements
        Utilities
        Libraries
        Window Managers
    Libraries
    Networking
        Admin
        Daemons
        News
        Utilities
    Development
        Debuggers
        Libraries
            Libc
        Languages
            Fortran
            Tcl
        Building
        Version Control
        Tools
    Shells
    Games
```

9.6.4 Prep

This is the second section in the spec file. It is used to get the sources ready to build. Here you need to do anything necessary to get the sources patched and setup like they need to be setup to do a `make`.

One thing to note: Each of these sections is really just a place to execute shell scripts. You could simply make an `sh` script and put it after the `%prep` tag to unpack and patch your sources. We have made macros to aid in this, however.

The first of these macros is the `%setup` macro. In its simplest form (no command line options), it simply unpacks the sources and `cd`'s into the source directory. It also takes the following options:

- `-n name` will set the name of the build directory to the listed `name`. The default is `$NAME-$VERSION`. Other possibilities include `$NAME`, `${NAME}${VERSION}`, or whatever the main tar file uses.
- `-c` will create and cd to the named directory *before* doing the untar.
- `-b #` will untar Source# *before* cd'ing into the directory (and this makes no sense with `-c` so don't do it). This is only useful with multiple source files.
- `-a #` will untar Source# *after* cd'ing into the directory.
- `-T` This option overrides the default action of untarring the Source and requires a `-b 0` or `-a 0` to get the main source file untarred. You need this when there are secondary sources.
- `-D` Do *not* delete the directory before unpacking. This is only useful where you have more than one setup macro. It should *only* be used in setup macros *after* the first one (but never in the first one).

The next of the available macros is the `%patch` macro. This macro helps automate the process of applying patches to the sources. It takes several options, listed below:

- `#` will apply Patch# as the patch file.
- `-p #` specifies the number of directories to strip for the patch(1) command.

- `-P` The default action is to apply `Patch` (or `Patch0`). This flag inhibits the default action and will require a `0` to get the main source file untarred. This option is useful in a second (or later) `%patch` macro that required a different number than the first macro.
- You can also do `%patch#` instead of doing the real command: `%patch # -P`

That should be all the macros you need. After you have those right, you can also do any other setup you need to do via `sh` type scripting. Anything you include up until the `%build` macro (discussed in the next section) is executed via `sh`. Look at the example above for the types of things you might want to do here.

9.6.5 Build

There aren't really any macros for this section. You should just put any commands here that you would need to use to build the software once you had untarred the source, patched it, and cd'ed into the directory. This is just another set of commands passed to `sh`, so any legal `sh` commands can go here (including comments). Your current working directory is reset in each of these sections to the top level of the source directory, so keep that in mind. You can `cd` into subdirectories if necessary.

9.6.6 Install

There aren't really any macros here, either. You basically just want to put whatever commands here that are necessary to install. If you have `make install` available to you in the package you are building, put that here. If not, you can either patch the makefile for a `make install` and just do a `make install` here, or you can hand install them here with `sh` commands. You can consider your current directory to be the top level of the source directory.

9.6.7 Optional pre and post Install/Uninstall Scripts

You can put scripts in that get run before and after the installation and uninstallation of binary packages. A main reason for this is to do things like run `ldconfig` after installing or removing packages that contain shared libraries. The macros for each of the scripts is as follows:

- `%pre` is the macro to do pre-install scripts.
- `%post` is the macro to do post-install scripts.
- `%preun` is the macro to do pre-uninstall scripts.
- `%postun` is the macro to do post-uninstall scripts.

The contents of these sections should just be any `sh` style script, though you do *not* need the `#!/bin/sh`.

9.6.8 Files

This is the section where you *must* list the files for the binary package. RPM has no way to know what binaries get installed as a result of `make install`. There is *NO* way to do this. Some have suggested doing a `find` before and after the package install. With a multiuser system, this is unacceptable as other files may be created during a package building process that have nothing to do with the package itself.

There are some macros available to do some special things as well. They are listed and described here:

- `%doc` is used to mark documentation in the source package that you want installed in a binary install. The documents will be installed in `/usr/doc/$NAME-$VERSION-$RELEASE`. You can list multiple documents on the command line with this macro, or you can list them all separately using a macro for each of them.
- `%config` is used to mark configuration files in a package. This includes files like sendmail.cf, passwd, etc. If you later uninstall a package containing config files, any unchanged files will be removed and any changed files will get moved to their old name with a `.rpmsave` appended to the filename. You can list multiple files with this macro as well.
- `%dir` marks a single directory in a file list to be included as being owned by a package. By default, if you list a directory name *WITH-*

OUT a `%dir` macro, *EVERYTHING* in that directory is included in the file list and later installed as part of that package.

The biggest caveat in the file list is listing directories. If you list `/usr/bin` by accident, your binary package will contain *every* file in `/usr/bin` on your system.

9.6.9 Building It

The Source Directory Tree

The first thing you need is a properly configured build tree. This is configurable using the `/etc/rpmrc` file. Most people will just use `/usr/src`.

You may need to create the following directories to make a build tree:

- `BUILD` is the directory where all building occurs by RPM. You don't have to do your test building anywhere in particular, but this is where RPM will do it's building.
- `SOURCES` is the directory where you should put your original source tar files and your patches. This is where RPM will look by default.
- `SPECS` is the directory where all spec files should go.
- `RPMS` is where RPM will put all binary RPMs when built.
- `SRPMS` is where all source RPMs will be put.

Test Building

The first thing you'll probably want to to is get the source to build cleanly without using RPM. To do this, unpack the sources, and change the directory name to $NAME.orig. Then unpack the source again. Use this source to build from. Go into the source directory and follow the instructions to build it. If you have to edit things, you'll need a patch. Once you get it to build, clean the source directory. Make sure and remove any files that get made from a `./configure`. Then `cd` back out of the source directory to its parent. Then you'll do something like:

```
diff -uNr dirname.orig dirname > ../SOURCES/dirname-linux.patch
```

This will create a patch for you that you can use in your spec file. Note that the "linux" that you see in the patch name is just an identifier. You might want to use something more descriptive like "config" or "bugs" to describe *why* you had to make a patch. It's also a good idea to look at the patch file you are creating before using it to make sure no binaries were included by accident.

Generating the File List

Now that you have source that will build and you know how to do it, build it and install it. Look at the output of the install sequence and build your file list from that to use in the spec file. We usually build the spec file in parallel with all of these steps. You can create the initial one and fill in the easy parts, and then fill in the other steps as you go.

Building the Package with RPM

Once you have a spec file, you are ready to try and build your package. The most useful way to do it is with a command like the following:

```
rpm -ba -v foobar-1.0.spec
```

There are other options useful with the `-b` switch as well:

- `p` means just run the `prep` section of the specfile.
- `l` is a list check that does some checks on `%files`.
- `c` do a prep and compile. This is useful when you are unsure of whether your source will build at all. It seems useless because you might want to just keep playing with the source itself until it builds and then start using RPM, but once you become accustomed to using RPM you will find instances when you will use it.
- `i` do a prep, compile, and install.
- `b` prep, compile, install, and build a binary package only.

- `a` build it all (both source and binary packages).

There are several modifiers to the `-b` switch. They are as follows:

- `--short-circuit` will skip straight to a specified stage (can only be used with c and i).
- `--clean` removes the build tree when done.
- `--keep-temps` will keep all the temp files and scripts that were made in /tmp. You can actually see what files were created in /tmp using the `-v` option.
- `--test` does not execute any real stages, but does keep-temp.
- `--time-check #` is very useful. By default, the time-check value is 7200 seconds (two hours). What this does is check all the files in `%files` and warns you if they are more than `#` seconds old (or the default). This lets you make sure that the newly created binaries are getting installed and not old ones that just happen to be still lying around. This author can attest to the value of this feature after having to release several RPP updates because old binaries were accidentally included. You can also turn this off (useful when building binary only packages of commercial software) by setting the value to zero.

9.6.10 Testing It

Once you have a source and binary rpm for your package, you need to test it. The easiest and best way is to use a totally different machine from the one you are building on to test. After all, you've just done a lot of `make install`'s on your own machine, so it should be installed fairly well.

You can do an `rpm -u packagename` on the package to test, but that can be deceiving because in building the package, you did a `make install`. If you left something out of your file list, it will not get uninstalled. You'll then reinstall the binary package and your system will be complete again, but your rpm still isn't. Make sure and keep in mind that just because you do a `rpm -ba package`, most people installing your package will just be doing the `rpm -i package`. Make sure you don't do anything in the `build` or `install` sections that will need to be done when the binaries are installed by themselves.

9.6.11 What to do with your new RPMs

Once you've made your own RPM of something (assuming its something that hasn't already been RPM'ed), you can contribute your work to others (also assuming you RPM'ed something freely distributable). To do so, you'll want to upload it to an FTP site somewhere. We hope RPM will become a standard that everyone starts using. If that is the case, you should probably upload your RPMs to sunsite.unc.edu. Until that time, please upload them to the Red Hat ftp site `ftp.redhat.com/pub/Incoming` or an official Red Hat mirror.

9.7 Advanced RPM Building

RPM has some very advanced features available for larger, more complex packages. It has the ability to build and output multiple binary subpackages. An example of this is the ability to produce separate Tcl/Tk binary packages from one spec file. Another example is the ability to use one spec file to create a single XFree86 package with no servers, and a separate package for each of the servers.

9.7.1 How to Get Started

The best way to get started is to look at an example spec file. The following tcl/tk spec file is a good one to start with (though you can also view the spec file of any package by installing the sources and looking in `/usr/src/redhat/SPECS`):

```
%package tcl
Description: Tool Command Language
Name: tcltk
Version: 7.4_4.0
Release: 1
Icon: tcl.gif
Source0: ftp.cs.berkeley.com:/pub/tcl/tcl7.4.tar.Z
Source1: ftp.cs.berkeley.com:/pub/tcl/tk4.0.tar.Z
Copyright: BSD
Group: Development/Languages/Tcl
Patch0: sunsite.unc.edu:/pub/Linux/devel/tcl7.4-1.diff.gz
```

```
Patch1: sunsite.unc.edu:/pub/Linux/devel/tk4.0-1.diff.gz
%package tk
Icon: tk.gif
Description: Tk toolkit
Group: Development/Languages/Tcl

%prep
%setup -T -c -a 0
%setup -T -D -a 1
%patch0 -p0
%patch1 -p0

%build
cd tcl7.4
./configure --prefix=/usr
make
cd ../tk4.0
./configure --prefix=/usr
make

%install
cd tcl7.4
make install
ln -sf libtcl7.4.a /usr/lib/libtcl.a
ln -sf libtcl7.4.so.1 /usr/lib/libtcl.so.1
ln -sf libtk4.0.a /usr/lib/libtk.a
ln -sf libtk4.0.so.1 /usr/lib/libtk.so.1
cd ../tk4.0
make install

%post tcl
/sbin/ldconfig

%post tk
/sbin/ldconfig

%postun tcl
/sbin/ldconfig

%postun tk
/sbin/ldconfig

%files tcl
/usr/lib/libtcl7.4.a
```

```
/usr/lib/libtcl.a
/usr/lib/libtcl7.4.so.1
/usr/lib/libtcl.so.1
/usr/include/tcl/tcl*
/usr/bin/tclsh
/usr/bin/tclsh7.4
/usr/lib/tcl7.4
/usr/man/man1/*tcl
/usr/man/man3/*tcl

%files tk
/usr/lib/libtk4.0.a
/usr/lib/libtk.a
/usr/lib/libtk4.0.so.1
/usr/lib/libtk.so.1
/usr/include/tcl/ks_names.h
/usr/include/tcl/default.h
/usr/include/tcl/tk*
/usr/lib/tk4.0
/usr/man/man1/*tk
/usr/man/man3/*tk
/usr/bin/wish
/usr/bin/wish4.0
```

9.7.2 Sub-Packages

One of the main advanced features of RPM is the ability to build sub-packages. They are easy to build as for most macros you can just add the subpackage name as a parameter for anything specific to a subpackage (and if you leave it off the section will apply to the main package).

9.7.3 The Header

The header only has one major difference, the `%package` macro. This macro is used in the header to tell which subpackage name to match the description with. If you omit the macro in the initial part of the header, you will get a main package with no change to the name. In the XFree86 package, however, there is no `%package` macro in the top of the header. This is because we wanted a base XFree86 package with all the common stuff in it and then several subpackages (XFree86-SVGA, etc.) with the servers.

Tcl/Tk does not need a main package, so the macro is at the top.

Another difference is the fact that this package has multiple source and patch lines. If you'll notice, there is now a `Source0` line instead of just `Source`. They are functionally equivalent, though it is a good idea to use `Source0` when there is more than one source file (and the same applies to patches as well).

9.7.4 Prep

Prep is basically the same as in the simple example, except it uses more of the options available to the setup and patch macros.

9.7.5 Build

Build is basically the same, with the exception that the setup macro above used the `-T` option. Because of this, you have to do a manual `cd` to get into the source directory.

You will also notice that the build does a `configure` before it can build. This is the section where any of this type of configuration should go.

9.7.6 Install

Again, everything is pretty normal with the exception of the fact that you must manually `cd` into the source directories.

9.7.7 Optional pre and post Install/Uninstall Scripts

This section is almost the same as in a simple RPM case (see the above section). It has two post install scripts that run ldconfig for each of the subpackages upon install. It *should* have two post uninstall scripts to run ldconfig as well.

9.7.8 Files

Here you will declare which files go in which packages. You really have multiple file sections, each started with a new `%files` macro and the name of the subpackage (except in the case where you have a main package...that `%files` macro will have no argument given to it). The other macros (doc, config, etc) work exactly the same as in the simple case.

You also have the option to use the `*` to glob filenames out of a directory. You need to be careful with this (perhaps test it first) so as not to include files you didn't mean to. The above example does this with the man pages.

9.7.9 What Now?

Please see the above sections on Testing and What to do with new RPMs. We want all the RPMs available we can get, and we want them to be good RPMs. Please take the time to test them well, and then take the time to upload them for everyone's benefit. Also, *please* make sure you are only uploading *freely available software*. Commercial software and shareware should *not* be uploaded unless they have a copyright expressly stating that this is allowed.

9.8 Multi-architectural RPM Building

RPM can now be used to build packages for the Intel i386, the Digital Alpha running Linux, and the Sparc. It has been reported to work on SGI's and HP workstations as well. There are several features that make building packages on all platforms easy. The first of these is the "optflags" directive in the `/etc/rpmrc`. It can be used to set flags used when building software to architecture specific values. Another feature is the "arch" macros in the spec file. They can be used to do different things depending on the architecture you are building on. Another feature is the "Exclude" directive in the header.

9.8.1 Sample spec File

The following is the spec file for the "zoneinfo" package. It is setup to build on both the Alpha and the Intel.

```
Description: Time zone utilities and data
Name: zoneinfo
Version: 95e
Release: 2
Copyright: Distributable
Group: Utilities/System
Source0: elsie.nci.nih.gov:/pub/tzcode95e.tar.gz
Source1: elsie.nci.nih.gov:/pub/tzdata95i.tar.gz
Patch0: zoneinfo-95e-make.patch
Patch1: zoneinfo-95e-64bit.patch

%prep
%setup -c -a 1
%patch0 -p1

%ifarch axp
%patch1 -p1
%endif

%build
make RPM_OPT_FLAGS="${RPM_OPT_FLAGS}"

%install
rm -rf /usr/lib/zoneinfo

make install

rm -f /usr/lib/zoneinfo/localtime
ln -sf ../../../etc/localtime /usr/lib/zoneinfo/localtime
ln -sf localtime /usr/lib/zoneinfo/posixrules
ln -sf localtime /usr/lib/zoneinfo/posixtime

strip /usr/sbin/zic /usr/sbin/zdump

%files
%doc README Theory
/usr/lib/zoneinfo
/usr/lib/libz.a
```

```
/usr/sbin/zic
/usr/sbin/zdump
/usr/man/man3/newctime.3
/usr/man/man3/newtzset.3
/usr/man/man5/tzfile.5
/usr/man/man8/zdump.8
/usr/man/man8/zic.8
```

9.8.2 Optflags

In this example, you see how the "optflags" directive is used from the `/etc/rpmrc`. Depending on which architecture you are building on, the proper value is given to `RPM_OPT_FLAGS`. You must patch the Makefile for your package to use this variable in place of the normal directives you might use (like `-m486` and `-O2`). You can get a better feel for what needs to be done by installing this source package and then unpacking the source and examine the Makefile. Then look at the patch for the Makefile and see what changes must be made.

9.8.3 Macros

The `%ifarch` macro is very important to all of this. Most times you will need to make a patch or two that is specific to one architecture only. In this case, RPM will allow you to apply that patch to just one architecture only.

In the above example, zoneinfo has a patch for 64 bit machines. Obviously, this should only be applied on the Alpha at the moment. So, we add an `%ifarch` macro around the 64 bit patch like so:

```
%ifarch axp
%patch1 -p1
%endif
```

This will insure that the patch is not applied on any architecture except the alpha.

9.8.4 Excluding Architectures from Packages

So that you can maintain source RPMs in one directory for all platforms, we have implemented the ability to "exclude" packages from being built on certain architectures. This is so you can still do things like

```
rpm --rebuild /usr/src/SRPMS/*.rpm
```

and have the right packages build. If you haven't yet ported an application to a certain platform, all you have to do is add a line like:

```
Exclude: axp
```

to the header of the spec file of the source package. Then rebuild the package on the platform that it does build on. You'll then have a source package that builds on an Intel and can easily be skipped on an Alpha.

9.8.5 Finishing Up

Using RPM to make multi-architectural packages is usually easier to do than getting the package itself to build both places. As more of the hard packages get built this is getting much easier, however. As always, the best help when you get stuck building an RPM is to look a similar source package.

Chapter 10

Control Panel

The control-panel is a launching pad for a number of different system administration tools. They make your life easier by letting you configure things without remembering configuration file formats and awkward command line options.

To start the control-panel, start the X Window System as root with `startx` and type `control-panel` in an xterm. You will need to be root to run the control-panel tools successfully. You can do this as well if you already have X running as a normal user. Just type `su -c control-panel` and then type the root password when prompted. If you plan to do other tasks as root, you could type `su -` followed by the root password when prompted. You will then be given a root shell. Here, you will need to type `DISPLAY=:0 control-panel &` to get the control panel to work. The "DISPLAY" part tells the control panel to use your display. This syntax works only for a Bourne-compatible shell like bash. If you run tcsh, you would enter `setenv DISPLAY :0; control-panel &`.

Double clicking on an icon starts up a tool. Please note that you are not prevented from starting two instances of any tool, but doing so is a *very bad idea* because you may try to edit the same files in two places and end up overwriting your own changes. If you do accidentally start a second copy of a tool, you should quit it immediately. Also, do not manually edit any files managed by the control-panel tools while the tools are running. Similarly, do not run any other programs that may change those files while the tools are running.

10.1 User and Group Configuration

The tool shown in Figure 10.1 manages the users and groups on your system. In a sense, it is a graphical editor for `/etc/passwd` and `/etc/group`. With this tool you can add and remove users and groups, set login shells, full names, home directories, uid, gids, etc.

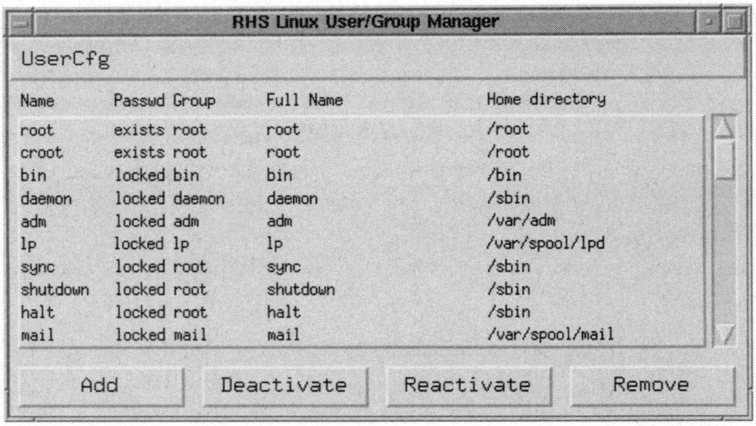

Figure 10.1: User and Group Configuration Panel

10.1.1 Adding a User

To add a user, click on the **Add** button in the main window. A dialog box will pop up like the on in figure 10.2 will appear, with some defaults already filled in.

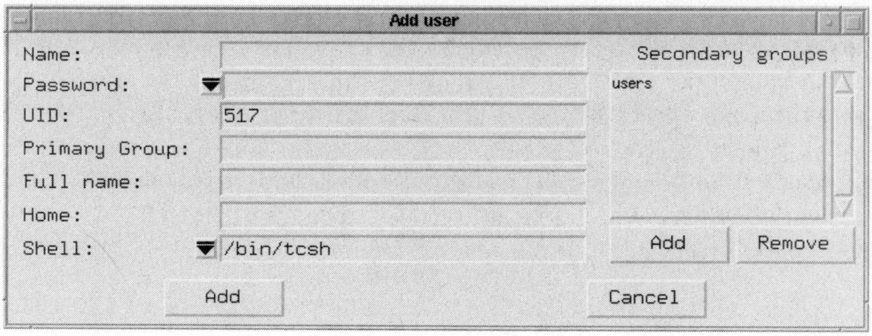

Figure 10.2: Add User Dialog Box

First enter the user name. This is *not* the user's first and last name, it is the id they will use to log on to the system. Do not include any spaces or colons, and do not enter more than 8 characters. Press the enter key when you are finished, and some of the other fields will be filed in with default values. You may change them if you wish, but there is no need to. Next, enter the user's full name, and select a login shell using the drop-down menu. And finally you need to do something with the password. There are three options here, Edit, None, or Lock. None is a very bad option — with no password anyone can login to your system using this id. Choosing Lock will prevent anyone from logging in with this id. Usually you will choose Edit. A small dialog box will appear where you will need to enter a password, and the confirm it by typing it a second time. Click on **Ok** after this, and then click on **Add** in the user entry dialog box to add the user.

If this user does not already have a home directory (and they won't unless you have already created one), you will be asked if you want to create one. Unless you will be mounting home directories from another machine, you should click on **Yes**.

10.1.2 Removing a User

To remove a user, select a user in the main window by clicking on it, and then click on **Remove**. After confirming the removal, you will be asked if you wish to remove the user's home directory and mail spool. You will normally answer **Yes**. After these files are deleted, you will be asked if you want to search the entire file system for files that have been "orphaned" by the removal of this user. Orphaned files are those that are not owned by any user in `/etc/passwd`. Since you have just removed a user from `/etc/passwd` any file that user owned will now be orphaned (except the home directory and mail spool, if you deleted them). If you answer yes, the search will proceed in the background, and all files found will be `chown`-ed to `nobody`. To find these files, execute the following command:

```
find / \( -group nobody -o -user nobody \) -print
```

Deactivating a User

Sometimes you may just want to temporarily "remove" a user, with the intention of reinstating the user later. The **Deactivate** and **Reactivate** functions handle this. When you deactivate a user, the user's password is locked by prepending a "*" to it, preventing the user from logging in. You also have the option of "collapsing" the user's home directory with `tar` and `gzip`, which can save some space. When you reactivate a user, the password locking is removed, and if the home directory was collapsed, it is expanded back to normal.

10.1.3 Creating a New Group

To create a new group, first switch to group editing mode by selecting **Edit groups** from the menu. Clicking on **Add** brings up a dialog box to specify the group details. First enter a name for the new group. Just like a user name, the group name should have no spaces or colons, and should be no longer than 8 characters. To add members to the group, click on the **Add** button on the left. A list of user names will appear from which you can select the group members. When you have selected all the group members, click on **Add**, then click on the lower **Add** button.

10.2 File System Configuration

The file system configuration tool shown in Figure 10.3 allows you to easily examine and manipulate file system mount points, types, options, etc. It is very useful for manipulating a large number of file systems. You probably don't want to do this unless you are an experienced system administrator. If you do know what you are doing, it should be fairly straightforward as to how to mount, unmount, and add devices.

The **Reload** entry in the **FSM** menu causes the file system configuration tool to re-load `/etc/fstab` from your hard drive. If you edit `/etc/fstab` by hand while the file system configuration tool is running (which you shouldn't do), you probably want to reload.

To use the buttons along the bottom of the window, select a filesystem in the main window, and click on one of the buttons. The buttons perform the following functions:

Info Displays information on the filesystem, including the device, partition type, filesystem type, mount point and options. comment, size, percent used, etc.

Check Performs a filesystem check (`fsck`) on the partition. You can only do this on *unmounted* partitions — if the partition is mounted, you will get an error and you will have to unmount it first.

Mount Mounts the selected filesystem.

Unmount Unmounts the selected filesystem.

Format Creates a new filesystem on the selected partition. This will erase all data on the selected partition! You can only do this on *unmounted* partitions — if the partition is mounted, you will get an error and you will have to unmount it first.

Edit Brings up a dialog box where you can edit the mount point, mount options, comment, etc.

10.2.1 Adding NFS Mounts

To mount a filesystem via NFS, select **Add Mount** from the **NFS** menu. A dialog box will appear and you will have to fill in the following values:

Device Enter the host name and path, separated by a colon. For example, `foo.bar.com:/usr/exported` indicates the `/usr/exported` directory on `foo.bar.com`.

Mount Point Enter the directory on your machine where you want to mount the NFS filesystem. For example, `/mnt/foo`.

Options Enter the mount options for this filesystem. The default is `soft,intr,rw`. The `rw` means is read-write, and `soft,intr` are options that make your system a little more resilient when the remote server goes down. See the mount man page for a complete list of available options.

Comment This optional field can be used to store a small comment.

After filling everything out properly, click on **OK**. At this point the entry is made in your `/etc/fstab`, but the filesystem is not actually mounted. To mount it, select it in the main window and click on **Mount**.

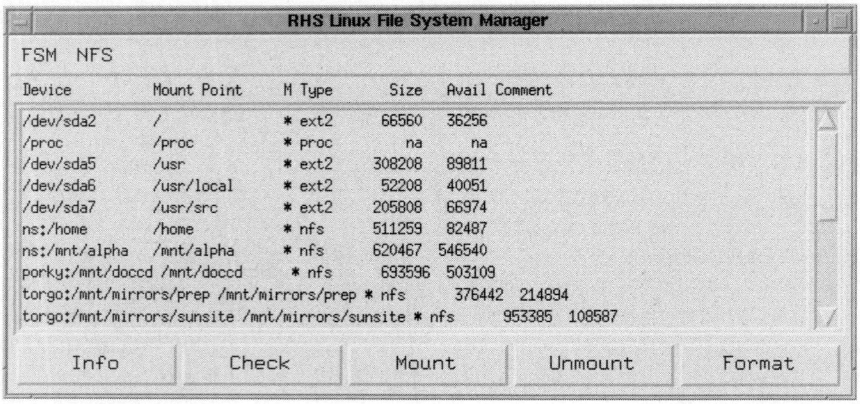

Figure 10.3: File System Configuration Panel

10.3 Printer Configuration

The printer configuration tool maintains `/etc/printcap`, print spool directories, and print filters. The filters are designed to use GhostScript (`gs`) and `nenscript` to allow you to print plain text as well as PostScript files.

While configuring your printers, keep in mind that `lpr` prints to the printer named `lp` by default. You will probably want `lp` to be one of your printer queue names.

Needless to say, ghostscript and nenscript should be installed.

To add a new printer, click on **Add**. This will bring up a dialog box where you indicate if you are adding a remote printer, or a local one. If your printer is connected to your machine's parallel or serial port select local, if it is somewhere on the network select remote. The printer configuration tool maintains `/etc/printcap`,

For a local printer, you need to fill in the following values:

Names Enter the names you want to give to this printer (queue). You can have multiple names, separated by a "`|`" character, eg, `lp|lp0|PostScript`.

Spool Directory Enter a unique directory to hold documents queued for printing on this printer. For example, `/var/spool/lpd/lp0`.

File Limit If you want to limit the size of documents printed, enter a size in KB here. A 0 indicates no limit.

Printer Device This is the physical device to which your printer is connected. For example, `/dev/lp1`.

Input Filter If you have a custom filter, enter the file name (full path) here. Otherwise, you should click on **Select**. This will bring up a dialog box where you select your **Printer Type**, **Resolution**, **Paper Size**, and you indicate if your printer requires an **EOF** character to be sent to it at the end of each job (many printers used under DOS require this).

Suppress Headers If you select this, no header pages will be printed for each job.

For a remote printer, you will fill in the following values:

Names See local printer.

Spool Directory See local printer.

File Limit See local printer.

Remote Host Enter the host name of the machine that has the printer. For example, `printer.foo.com`.

Remote Queue Enter the name of the queue on the remote machine for the remote printer. For example, `PostScript`.

Click on **Ok** and your new printer is added. Some versions of the `lpd` printer daemon may need to be restarted before they will recognize the new printer. To do this select **Restart lpd** from the **lpd** menu.

10.4 Network Configuration

The network configuration panel shown in figure 10.4 is designed to allow easy manipulation of parameters such as IP address, gateway address, network address, etc, as well as name servers and `/etc/hosts`. Network devices can be added, removed, configured, brought up, brought down, etc. Ethernet, loopback and SLIP/PPP devices are supported. SLIP/PPP support works fine on most hardware, but some hardware setups do exhibit unpredictable behavior.

10.4.1 Adding an Ethernet Device

If you have added an Ethernet card to your machine since you installed, or you didn't set your Ethernet card up at install time, you can configure it by clicking on **Add** in the **Interfaces** panel. This will being up a window where you need to click on `ethernet` and enter a device name. The device name should be something like `eth0`, or `eth1` if this is your second Ethernet device. Click on **OK** after doing this.

In the next window you have to fill in the following parameters:

Ethernet Device This is already filled in – it is the device you entered in the previous window.

IP Address Enter an IP address for your Ethernet device.

Netmask Enter the network mask for your Ethernet.

Network Enter the network address for your Ethernet.

Broadcast Enter the broadcast address for your Ethernet.

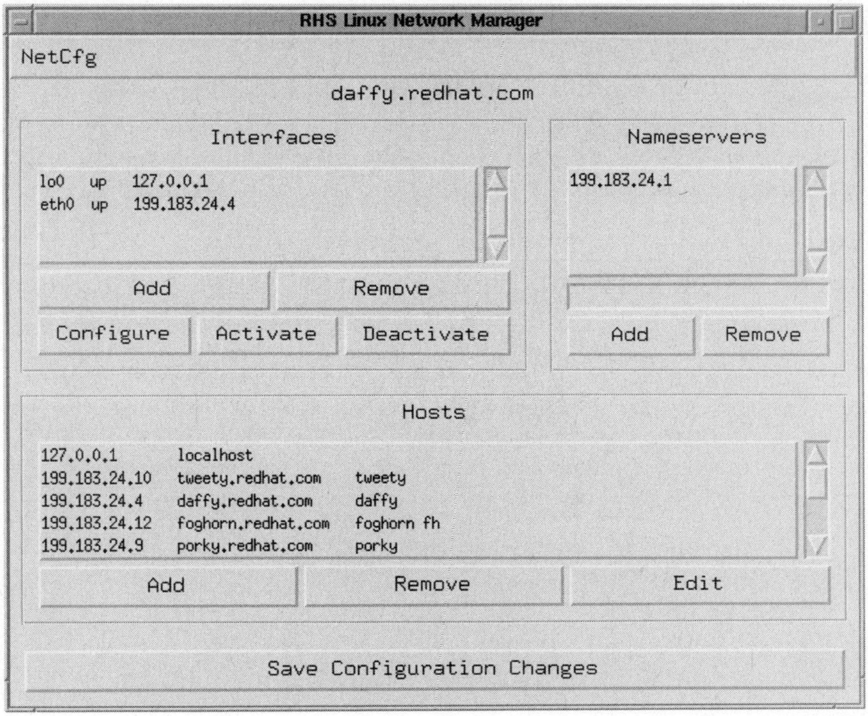

Figure 10.4: Network Configuration Panel

Gateway If you have a gateway, enter its IP address here. If you don't have a gateway, enter `none`.

Activate at Boot If you want the device to be configured automatically when your machine boots (usually a good idea), select this by clicking on the box.

After filling everything in, click on **OK**. The device should then appear in you **Interfaces** list, but it is not currently active (it says "down"). To activate it it click on **Activate**. If it does not come up properly, you may need to reconfigure it by clicking on **Configure**.

10.4.2 Adding a SLIP or PPP Device

To configure SLIP or PPP for your machine, click on **Add** in the **Interfaces** panel. This will being up a window where you need to click on `slip` or `ppp` and enter a device name. The device name should be something like `sl0` or `ppp0`, *not* your modem device! Click on **OK** after doing this.

In the next window you have to fill in the following parameters (these are for SLIP – PPP is similar):

SLIP Device This is already filled in – it is the device you entered in the previous window.

Local IP Address Enter an IP address for your machine's SLIP device. Leave this blank if your ISP uses dynamic addressing (this will require that you edit `/etc/dip-script` to comment out the `get $local` line.)

DIP Script You should enter `/etc/dip-script`, unless you want to make a custom script, or have more than one SLIP or PPP device.

Remote IP Address Enter the IP address of the machine you are connecting to.

Modem Speed Enter your modem speed (eg `28800`).

Phone Number Enter the phone number to call up the remote machine.

Login Name Enter the name with which to log in to the remote machine.

Password Enter the password you need to log in to the remote machine.

Connect String Enter the string your modem sends when the connection is made (eg. `ing...`).

Connection Type Enter the type of connection you want to make. For a SLIP device this is either `SLIP` or `CSLIP` (for a PPP device use `PPP`).

Activate at Boot If you want the device to be configured automatically when your machine boots select this by clicking on the box.

Restart If you select this a small script will be executed that watches the connection to make sure it is active. If the connection goes down, the script will try to re-establish it.

After filling everything in, click on **OK**. The device should then appear in your **Interfaces** list, but it is not currently active (it says "down"). To activate it it click on **Activate**. If it does not come up properly, you may need to reconfigure it by clicking on **Configure**.

It is likely that you will have to edit `/etc/dip-script` a little to get everything to work. Unfortunately there is no way to automate this. You simply need to adjust it to talk to your SLIP or PPP server in the manner it expects. The things to pay attention to are the `wait` lines, which must recognize stuff your server returns.

Do not edit the `@@@......@@@` entries – those are automatically filled in with the values you just entered while configuring the device.

10.5 Time and Date

The time machine allows you to change the time and date by clicking on the appropriate part of the time and date display and clicking on the arrows to change the value.

The system clock is not changed until you click on the Set System Clock button.

Click on Reset Time to set the time machine time back to that of the system.

CAUTION: Changing the time can seriously confuse programs that depend on the normal progression of time, and could possibly cause problems. Try to quit as many applications and processes as possible before changing the time or date.

Chapter 11

Glint

Red Hat provides a graphical tool to aid in package installation and removal. It's called glint (Graphical Linux INstallation Tool) and runs under the X Windows System. It allows easy installation, uninstallation, upgrading, querying, and verification of packages. The interface is similar to the one found in many popular file managers and is simple to use.

Operations are performed in glint by selecting the packages to operate on and then selecting the operation to perform via pushbuttons. Installing a package places all of the components of that package on your system. Uninstalling one removes all traces of the package except for configuration files you have modified. Upgrading a package installs the newly available version and uninstalls all other versions that were previously installed. This allows quick upgrading to the latest releases of packages.

The query operation lets you examine the details of both installed or available package. You can view the description of the package, where and when it was built, the files in the package, and other attributes. All of the configuration and documentation components of each package are clearly marked as such to reduce the time you spend looking for them.

Using glint to perform all of these operations is the same as using rpm to do them from the command line. However, the graphical nature of glint often makes these operations easier to perform.

11.1 Starting glint

To start glint, simply run `glint &` from any X terminal window. That will bring up a window that looks like the one in figure 11.1. Any user can use glint to query and verify packages, but if you need to install, uninstall, or upgrade packages be sure to run glint as root.

There are two main parts to the glint interface. The first, on the left, allows you to browse and select the packages installed on your system. The right side contains buttons that manipulate the selected packages.

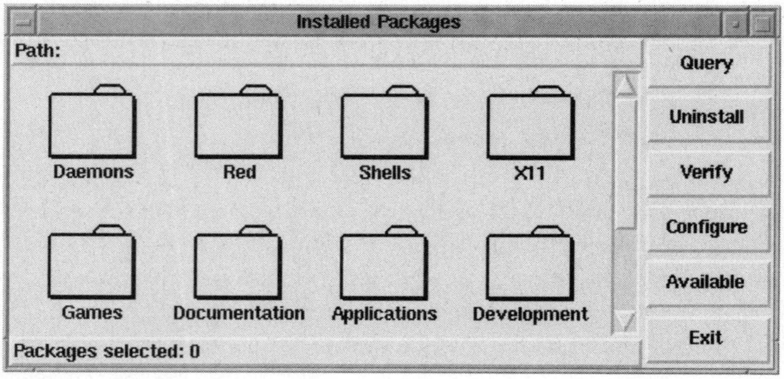

Figure 11.1: Main Glint Window

11.2 The Package Display

Each folder icon in glint represents a group of packages. Each group can contain other groups, which allows for flexible locations of packages. Groups are used to place packages which perform similar functions in similar locations. For example, Red Hat includes many application programs such as editors and spreadsheets. All of the text based ones appear in the "Applications" group. Inside of that group, there is another grouping for all of the editors that are shipped.

By convention, groups are written in the same way as UNIX paths. The top most group is written first, and subsequent groups follow with a slash separating the group names. This means that an X based drawing program appears in the X11/Applications/Graphics group.

To view the packages and subgroups within a group, double click the left mouse button on a group's folder icon. The window will then change to show what that package contains. The top line of the package display shows which group you're currently looking in, as well as the groups leading to the current one. To return to the previous group you were looking at, double click on the "Back" folder, which is always in the upper left hand corner of the folder area (though it often gets scrolled away).

If you'd like to examine a subgroup in a new window, double click the middle mouse button on its folder. If your mouse has only two buttons, click both. This will create a new window with that group in it.

11.2.1 Context Sensitive Menus

Pressing the right mouse button on any icon in the package window brings up a small, *context sensitive* menu. The exact items it contains depends on exactly where you press it. They all contain options to select or deselect the item, and many let you install, uninstall, query, upgrade, or verify the item you clicked on. There's more information on how to do these things later.

To choose an item from a context sensitive menu, press and hold the right mouse button on a icon. While still holding the right button down, move the mouse pointer over the item you'd like to select (which will then become highlighted). Release the right mouse button to select that item and make the menu disappear.

11.2.2 Selecting Packages

To select a single package, click the left mouse button on it. You'll notice a thin border appear around the package's icon (as shown in figure 11.2) which shows that it's currently selected. To unselect it, click the left mouse button on it and the border will disappear. The number of packages currently selected is always displayed at the bottom of the window. A group's folder icon displays the number of packages inside of that group have been selected, or `All` if all of them have been.

The context sensitive menu for a package also allows easy selection and

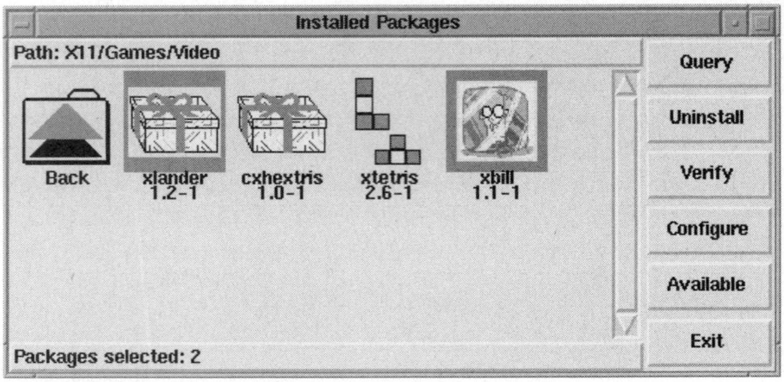

Figure 11.2: Selecting Packages in Glint

unselection. Using the `select` and `unselect` options on a package's icon selects or unselects that package, while those options on a group's folder icon select and unselect all of the packages in that group. Using these menu options makes selecting groups of packages much quicker than selecting each package individually.

11.2.3 Viewing Available Packages

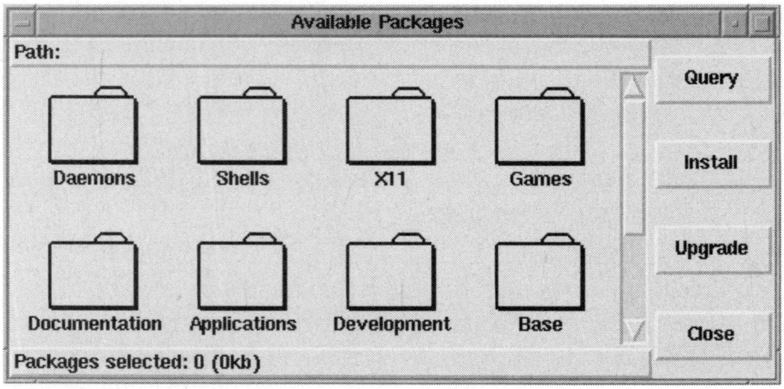

Figure 11.3: Available Window

To see what packages are available for you to install, choose the `Available` pushbutton from any glint window. After a few moments, a new window, like the one shown below in figure 11.3, will appear. The differences in the title and buttons indicate that this window is listing packages you may install. Navigating through these packages and selecting them is the same as in the other glint windows.

If you get an error message from glint saying that it can't find any RPMs, see the section below on Configuration.

11.3 Configuration

The only configuration information glint needs is the path to new RPMs. When you're using your Red Hat Linux CD-ROM, this will probably be /mnt/cdrom/RedHat/RPMS, which is the default path for glint. If you download new RPMs from the Internet or want to install RPMs via a NFS mounted CD-ROM this path will probably be different for you.

Figure 11.4: Configuration Window

To change this path, first be sure to close all of the windows listing available packages you may have open. Then choose the `Configuration` option from one of the remaining windows. This will open a dialog box like the one shown in figure 11.4. Here you can type the full path to the RPMs you'd like to look at. Choosing the `Save` button will save this path, making it the default for future glint sessions. The `Default` button restores the path to the one that glint used when it started.

After changing this path and closing the dialog box, you can use the `Available` button to view the packages available in the new location.

11.4 Package Manipulation

11.4.1 Querying Packages

The easiest way to query a single package or group is to use the query option from the icon's context sensitive menu. If you want to query a more diverse set of packages, select them all and use the `Query` button in one of the windows.

Using either of these methods creates a window like the one shown in figure 11.5. If you only choose one package, it will look a bit different however, so some of this won't apply.

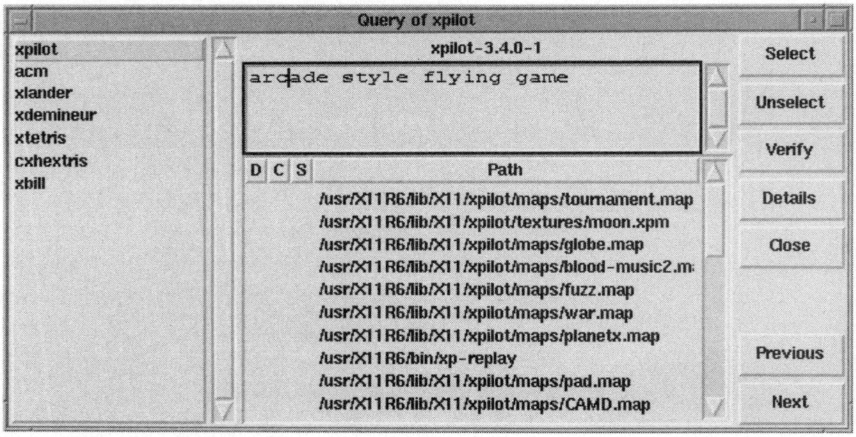

Figure 11.5: Query Window

On the very left of the window is a list of the packages that have been queried. Selecting one of them will change the information in the rest of the window. You may step through them in order by using the `Next` and `Previous` buttons on the right side of the window.

The name, version, and release of the current package are in the top middle of the query window. Immediately below this is the description of the package, which can be quite large. A scroll bar is there to let you read the whole thing.

Below the description is a list of the files contained in the package. Along with the full path to the file, the file list tells you a couple of other things. If a `D` appears to the left of the path, that file is a documentation file and would be a good thing to read. If a `C` appears there, then the file is a configuration file. A `*` means that the correct version of that file is not installed on your system. This can occur because a more recent version of a package was installed or two packages contain different version of the same file.

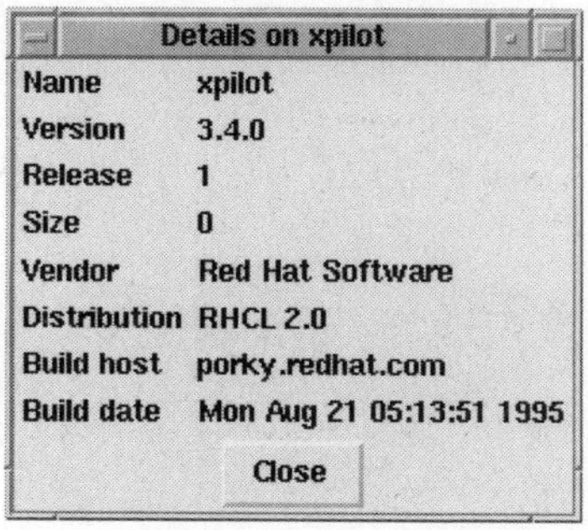

Figure 11.6: Query Details

More information on a package can be seen by clicking on the `Details` pushbutton. A window like the one in figure 11.6 will then appear. This lists more information about the package being displayed in the main query window. When you select a new package in the query window, the information in the details window will change to reflect your new choice.

You may also select, unselect, or verify a package while querying it by using the buttons provided. Click on the `Close` button when you are finished looking at the packages.

11.4.2 Verifying Packages

Verifying a package checks all of the files in the package to insure they match the ones present on your system. The checksum, file size, permissions, and owner attributes are all checked against the database. This check can be used when you suspect that one of programs files has become corrupted due to the installation of new programs.

Choosing the packages to verify is the same as choosing the packages to query. Select the packages and use the `Verify` button or choose the `Verify` entry from a context sensitive menu. A window opens like the one in figure 11.7.

Figure 11.7: Verify Window

The three columns in this window describe the package with a problem in it, the file that has the problem, and a brief description of the discrepancies that were found. While the check is running, the current file being checked appears as the last element in the list, and the problem is listed as `(checking)`. A full list of the problems that can be found through verification appears in figure 11.8.

Problem	Descrpition
missing	The file is no longer on your system
mode	permission bits have changed
size	file's size has changed
uid	owner's uid has changed
gid	owner's gid has changed
md5	the md5 checksum has changed
link	the file is a symlink to the wrong place

Figure 11.8: Possible Problems found by Verification

To get more information on the problems found with a file, double click on the file's path. A window like the one shown in figure 11.9 lists the expected and current values of the attributes that are amiss.

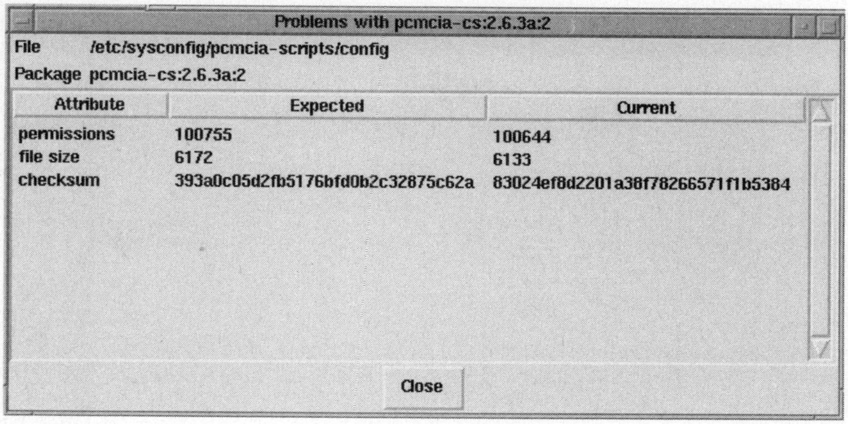

Figure 11.9: Verification Details

11.4.3 Installing New Packages

Installing new packages from glint is very simple. First look at the packages available for installation (see the section 11.2.3 for how to do this). You may select any number of these (and query them if you're not sure what they are) for installation in the same manner you select packages for verification. If you want to install a single package or group, the context sensitive menus provide a shortcut for doing so. Figure 11.10 shows a window with some packages selected for installation.

After you've begun the installation, a window appears like the one in figure 11.11. It tracks the progress of the installation so you'll know something is happening. The top bar shows how much of the current package (whose name is listed inside of it) has been installed while the bottom graph shows how much of the total installation has been finished. The number of packages, package sizes, and time estimates are continually updated.

If a problem occurs during the installation, a window will appear listing any errors that occurred. If this happens, you should correct the problems and then try again.

After the installation has completed, the package and groups that have been installed are moved from the available window to the main glint window to show you that they have been successfully installed.

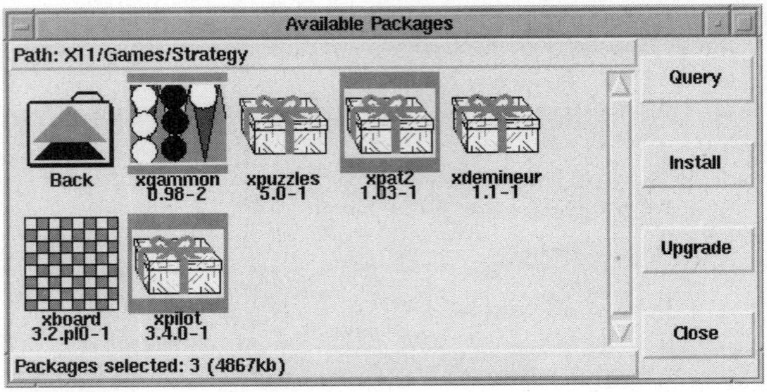

Figure 11.10: Packages Selected for Installation

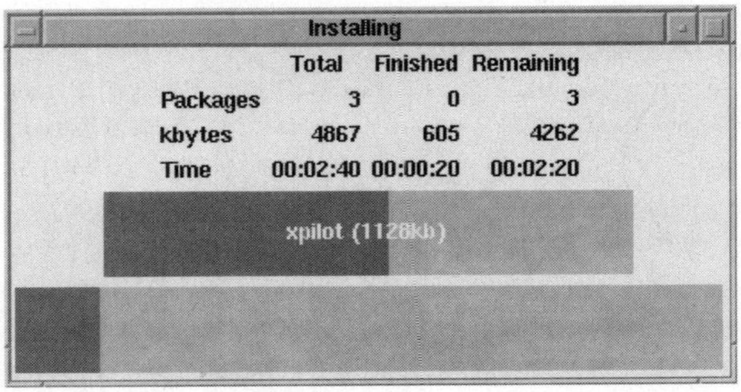

Figure 11.11: Installation Progress

Upgrading Packages

When a new version of a package has been released, it is easy to install it on your system. Select the packages from the window of available packages in the same way you select packages for installation. Both the `Upgrade` button and the context sensitive menus will begin the upgrade.

During the upgrade, you'll see a progress indicator like the one for installing packages. When it's finished, the installed packages will appear in the the main glint windows and any old versions of the packages will be removed.

It is much better to use the upgrade option than to uninstall the old versions of a package and then install the new one. Using upgrade ensures that any changes you made to package configuration files get preserved properly, while doing it manually could cause those changes to be lost.

If you run out of disk space during an installation, the install will fail. However, the package which was being installed when the error occurred may leave some files around. To clean this up, reinstall the package after you've made more disk space available.

11.4.4 Uninstalling Packages

Uninstalling a package is not the same as upgrading one. When a package is uninstalled, any files it uses that are not needed by other packages on your system are removed. Changed configuration files are copied to <filename>.rpmsave so you can reuse them later.

Like verifying and querying packages, you can remove a package through the buttons on the right of the glint window or through a context sensitive menu. Remember that when you make a choice from a group's menu, the operation is performed an all of the packages in that group, so be careful!

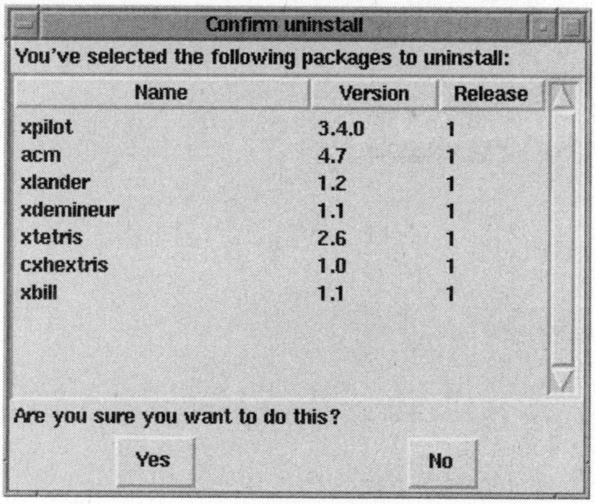

Figure 11.12: Uninstall Window

Once you've begun the uninstall, glint asks for confirmation, showing a window like the one in figure 11.12. All of the packages that are about to be uninstalled are listed. You should look at them all to insure you're not about to remove something you want to keep. Clicking the **Yes** button will start the uninstallation process. After it completes, the packages and groups that have been removed will disappear from any windows they were in.

Chapter 12

System Administration

This chapter is an overview of the RH Linux system. It will illustrate things that you may not know about the system and things that are somewhat different from other UNIX systems. Note that most system administration task are performed with the control-panel, which is covered in chapter 10.

12.1 Filesystem Structure

Red Hat Software is committed to the Linux File System Standard, a collaborative document that defines the names and locations of many files and directories. We will continue to track the standard to keep Red Hat compliant.

While compliance with the standard means many things, the two most important are compatibility with other compliant systems, and the ability to mount the `/usr` partition read-only. The `/usr` partition contains common executables and is not meant to be changed by users. Because of the, the `/usr` partition can be mounted from the CD-ROM or from another machine via read-only NFS. The current FSSTND standard document is the authoritative reference to any FSSTND compliant filesystem, but the standard leaves many areas undefined or extensible. In this section we provide an overview of the standard and a description of the parts of the filesystem not covered by the standard.

The complete standard can be viewed at:

`http://www.eg.bucknell.edu/~quinlan/fsstnd`

12.1.1 Overview of the FSSTND

The directories and files noted here are a small subset of those specified by the FSSTND document. Check the latest FSSTND document for the most up to date and complete information.

The `/etc` Directory

The `/etc` directory is reserved for configuration files that are local to your machine. No binaries are to put in `/etc` (binaries that were in the past put in `/etc` should now go into `/sbin` (or possibly `/bin`)).

The `X11` and `skel` directories should be subdirectories of `/etc`:

```
/etc
  |- X11
  +- skel
```

The `X11` directory is for X11 configuration files such as `XF86Config`. The `skel` directory is for "skeleton" user files, which are files used to populate a HOME directory when a user is first created.

The `/lib` Directory

The `/lib` directory should contain only those libraries that are need to execute the binaries in `/bin` and `/sbin`.

The `/sbin` Directory

The `/sbin` directory is for executables used only by the root user, and only those executables needed to boot and mount `/usr` and perform system recovery operations. The FSSTND says:

> "/sbin typically contains files essential for booting the system in addition to the binaries in /bin. Anything executed after /usr is known to be mounted (when there are no problems) should be placed in /usr/sbin. Local-only system administration binaries should be placed into /usr/local/sbin."

At a minimum, the following programs should be in `/sbin`:

```
clock, getty, init, update, mkswap, swapon, swapoff,
halt, reboot, shutdown, fdisk, fsck.*, mkfs.*, lilo,
arp, ifconfig, route
```

The `/usr` Directory

The `/usr` directory is for files that are shareable across a whole site. The `/usr` directory usually has its own partition, and it should be mountable read only. The following directories should be subdirectories of `/usr`:

```
/usr
  |- X11R6
  |- bin
  |- dict
  |- doc
  |- etc
  |- games
  |- include
  |- info
  |- lib
  |- local
  |- man
  |- sbin
  |- share
  +- src
```

The `X11R6` directory is for the X Window System (XFree86 on RH Linux), bin is for executables, doc is for random non-man-page documentation, etc is for site-wide configuration files, include is for C header files, info is for GNU info files, lib is for libraries, man is for man pages, sbin is for system administration binaries (those that do not belong in /sbin), and src is for source code.

The `/usr/local` Directory

The FSSTND says:

> "The /usr/local hierarchy is for use by the system administrator when installing software locally. It needs to be safe from being overwritten when the system software is updated. It may be used for programs and data that are shareable amongst a group of machines, but not found in /usr."

The `/usr/local` directory is similar in structure to the `/usr` directory. It has the following subdirectories, which are similar in purpose to those in the `/usr` directory:

```
/usr/local
      |- bin
      |- doc
      |- etc
      |- games
      |- include
      |- info
      |- lib
      |- man
      |- sbin
      +- src
```

The `/var` directory

Since the FSSTND requires that you be able to mount `/usr` read-only, any programs that write log files or need spool or lock directories probably should write them to the `/var` directory. The FSSTND says `/var` is for

> "... variable data files. This includes spool directories and files, administrative and logging data, and transient and temporary files."

The following directories should be subdirectories of `/var`:

```
/var
  |- log
  |- catman
  |- lib
  |- local
  |- named
  |- nis
  |- preserve
  |- run
  |- lock
  |- tmp
  +- spool
      |- at
      |- cron
      |- lpd
      |- mail
      |- mqueue
      |- rwho
      |- smail
      |- uucp
      +- news
```

System log files such as `wtmp` and `lastlog` go in `/ver/log`. The `/var/lib` directory also contains the rpm system databases. Formatted man pages got in `/var/catman`, and lock files go in `/var/lock`. The `/var/spool` directory has subdirectories for various systems that need to store data files.

12.1.2 `/usr/local` in RH Linux

In RH Linux, the intended use for `/usr/local` is slightly different from that specified by the FSSTND. The FSSTND says that `/usr/local` should be where your store software that is to remain safe from system software upgrades. Since system upgrades from RHS are done safely with the RPM system and Glint, you don't need to protect files by putting them in `/usr/local`. Instead, we recommend you use `/usr/local` for software that is local to your machine.

For instance, let's say you have mounted `/usr` via read-only NFS from *beavis*. If there is a package or program you would like to install, but are not allowed to write to *beavis*, you should install it under `/usr/local`. Later perhaps, if you've managed to convince the system administrator of *beavis* to install the program on `/usr`, you can uninstall it from `/usr/local`.

12.2 Special Red Hat File Locations

In addition to the files pertaining to the RPM system that reside in `/var/lib/rpm` (see chapter 9), there are two other special locations that are reserved for RH Linux configuration and operation.

The control-panel and related tools put lots of stuff in `/usr/lib/rhs`. There is probably nothing here that you would want to edit. It is mostly small scripts, bitmaps and text files.

The other location, `/etc/sysconfig`, stores configuration information. The major users of the files in this directory are the scripts that run at boot time. It is possible to edit these by hand, but it would be better to use the proper control-panel tool.

12.3 Users, Groups and User-Private Groups

Managing users and groups has traditionally been tedious. RH Linux has a few tools and conventions that make user and groups easier to manage, and more useful.

The easiest way to manage users and groups is through the Users and Groups module of the control-panel (see section 10 for details on the control-panel and section 10.1 for details on the Users and Groups module).

You can also use `adduser` to create a new user from the command line.

12.3.1 Standard Users

Table 12.3.1 lists the standard users set up by the installation process (this is essentially the `/etc/passwd` file). The group id (GID) in this table is the *primary group* for the user. See section 12.3.3 for details on how groups are used.

User	UID	GID	HOME Directory	Shell
root	0	0	/root	/bin/bash
bin	1	1	/bin	
daemon	2	2	/sbin	
adm	3	4	/var/adm	
lp	4	7	/var/spool/lpd	
sync	5	0	/sbin	/bin/sync
shutdown	6	0	/sbin	/sbin/shutdown
halt	7	0	/sbin	/sbin/halt
mail	8	12	/var/spool/mail	
news	9	13	/var/spool/news	
uucp	10	14	/var/spool/uucp	
operator	11	0	/root	/bin/bash
games	12	100	/usr/local/games	
gopher	13	30	/usr/lib/gopher-data	
ftp	14	50	/usr/rhs/ftp	
nobody	99	99	/root	

Figure 12.1: Standard Users

12.3.2 Standard Groups

Table 12.3.2 lists the standard groups as set up by the installation process (this is essentially the `/etc/group` file).

12.3.3 User Private Groups

RH Linux uses a user private group (UPG) scheme, which makes UNIX groups much easier to use. The UPG scheme does not add or change anything in the standard UNIX way of handling groups. It simply offers a new convention for handling groups. Whenever you create a new user, by default, he or she has a unique group. The scheme works as follows:

User Private Group Each user has it's own primary group, to which only it is a member.

Group	Group ID	Members
root	0	root
bin	1	root,bin,daemon
daemon	2	root,bin,daemon
sys	3	root,bin,adm
adm	4	root,adm,daemon
tty	5	
disk	6	root
lp	7	daemon,lp
mem	8	
kmem	9	
wheel	10	root
mail	12	mail
news	13	news
uucp	14	uucp
man	15	
games	20	
gopher	30	
dip	40	
ftp	50	ftp
nobody	99	
users	100	

Figure 12.2: Standard Groups

umask = 002 The traditional UNIX umask is 022, which prevents other users *and other members of a user's primary group* from modifying a user's files. Since every user has their own private group in the UPG scheme, this "group protection" is not needed. A umask of 002 will prevent users from modifying other users' private files. The umask is set in `/etc/profile`.

SGID bit on Directories By setting the SGID bit on a directory (with `chmod g+s` *directory*), files created in that directory will have their group set to the directory's group.

Most computing sites like to create a group for each major project and assign people to the groups they need to be in. Managing files traditionally has been difficult, though, because when someone creates a file it is owned by the primary group he or she belongs to. When a single person works on multiple projects, it becomes hard to make the files owned by the group that is associated with that project. The UPG scheme is a system in which groups are automatically assigned to files on a project-by-project basis, which makes managing group projects very simple.

Let's say you have a big project called *devel*, with many people editing the devel files in a `devel` directory. Make a group called `devel`, `chgrp` the `devel` directory to `devel`, and add the all the devel users to the `devel` group. Now, all the devel users will be able to edit the devel files and create new files in the `devel` directory, and these files will always retain their `devel` group. Thus, they will always be edit-able by other devel users.

If you have multiple projects like *devel*, and users who are working on multiple projects, these users will never have to change their umask or group when they move from project to project. The SGID bit on each project's main directory "selects" the proper group.

Since each user's HOME directory is owned by the user and their private group, it is safe to set the SGID bit on the HOME directory. However, by default, files are created with the primary group of the user, so the SGID bit would be redundant.

User Private Group Rationale

Since the UPG scheme is new, many people have questions about it, and they wonder why it is necessary. The following is the rationale for the scheme.

- You'd like to have a group of people work on a set of files in say, the `/usr/lib/emacs/site-lisp` directory. You trust a few people to mess around in there, but certainly not everyone.
- So you enter:

  ```
  chown -R root.emacs /usr/lib/emacs/site-lisp
  ```

  and you add the proper users to the group.
- To allow the users to actually create files in the directory you enter:

  ```
  chmod 775 /usr/lib/emacs/site-lisp
  ```

- But when a user creates a new file it is assigned the group of the users default group (usually `users`). To prevent this you enter

  ```
  chmod 2775 /usr/lib/emacs/site-lisp
  ```

  which causes everything in the directory to be created with the "emacs" group.
- But the new file needs to be mode 664 for another user in the emacs group to be able to edit it. To do this you make the default umask 002.
- Well, this all works fine, except that if your default group is "users", every file you create in your home directory will be writable by everybody in "users" (usually everyone).
- To fix this, you make each user have a "private group" as their default group.

At this point, by making the default umask 002 and giving everyone a private default group, you can easily set up groups that users can take advantage of without doing any magic. Just create the group, add the users, and do the above chown and chmod on the group's directories.

12.4 The Boot Process, Init, and Shutdown

12.4.1 System V Init

This section is a brief description of the internals of the boot up process. It basically covers in detail how the machine boots using SysV Init and the differences between the original Init used in older Linux releases.

Init is the program that gets run by the kernel at boot time. It is in charge of starting all the normal processes that need to run at boot time. These include the gettys that allow you to log in, NFS daemons, FTP daemons, and anything else you want to run when your machine boots.

System V init is fast becoming the standard in the Linux world to control the startup of software at boot time. This is because it is easier to use and more powerful and flexible than the traditional BSD init.

The init binary is located in `/sbin` and not `/etc`. This is important as one might try and upgrade a machine to System V init without re-installing and reformatting. The linux kernel looks in `/etc` for its init first, so you must make sure and delete your old init from there if any.

SYSV init also differs from BSD init in that the config files are in a subdirectory of `/etc` instead of residing directly in `/etc`. This directory is called `rc.d`. In there you will find `rc.sysinit` and the following directories:

- init.d
- rc0.d
- rc1.d
- rc2.d
- rc3.d
- rc4.d
- rc5.d
- rc6.d

`init.d` contains a bunch of scripts. Basically, you need one script for each service you may need to start at boot time or when entering another runlevel. Services include things like networking, nfs, sendmail, httpd, etc. Services do not include things like setserial that must only be run once and then exited. Things like that should go in `rc.local` or `rc.serial`.

`rc.local` should be in `/etc/rc.d` if you want one. Most systems include one even though it doesn't do much. You can also include an rc.serial in `/etc/rc.d` if you need to do serial port specific things at boot time.

The chain of events is as follows:

- the kernel looks in several places for `init` and runs the first one it finds
- `init` runs `/etc/rc.d/rc.sysinit`
- `rc.sysinit` does a bunch of necessary things and then runs `rc.serial` (if it exists)
- `init` runs all the scripts for the default runlevel.
- `init` runs `rc.local`

The default runlevel is decided in `/etc/inittab`. You should have a line close to the top like:

```
id:3:initdefault:
```

From this, you'd look in the second column and see that the default runlevel is 3, as should be the case for most systems. If you want to change it, you can edit `/etc/inittab` by hand and change the 3. Be very careful when you are messing with the inittab. If you do mess up, you can fix it by rebooting and doing:

```
LILO boot:  linux single
```

This *should* allow you to boot into single user mode so you can fix it.

Now, how does it run all the right scripts? If you do an `ls -l` on `rc3.d`, you might see something like:

```
lrwxrwxrwx 1 root root 17  13:11 S10network -> ../init.d/network
```

```
lrwxrwxrwx 1 root root 16  13:11 S30syslog -> ../init.d/syslog
lrwxrwxrwx 1 root root 14  13:32 S40cron -> ../init.d/cron
lrwxrwxrwx 1 root root 14  13:11 S50inet -> ../init.d/inet
lrwxrwxrwx 1 root root 13  13:11 S60nfs -> ../init.d/nfs
lrwxrwxrwx 1 root root 15  13:11 S70nfsfs -> ../init.d/nfsfs
lrwxrwxrwx 1 root root 18  13:11 S90lpd -> ../init.d/lpd.init
lrwxrwxrwx 1 root root 11  13:11 S99local -> ../rc.local
```

What you'll notice is that there are no real "files" in the directory. Everything there is a link to one of the scripts in the init.d directory. The links also have an "S" and a number at the beginning. The "S" means to start this particular script and a "K" would mean to stop it. The number is just there for ordering purposes. Init will start all the services based on the order they appear. You can duplicate numbers, but it will only confuse you somewhat. You just need to use a two digit number only, along with an upper case "S" or "K" to start or stop the services you need to.

How does it start and stop services? Simple. Each of the scripts is written to accept an argument which can be "start" and "stop". You can execute those scripts by hand in fact with a command like:

```
/etc/rc.d/init.d/httpd.init stop
```

to stop the httpd server. Init just reads the name and if it has a "K", it calls the script with the "stop" argument. If it has an "S" it calls the script with a "start" argument.

Why all these runlevels?

Some people want an easy way to setup machines to be multi-purpose. I could have a "server" runlevel that just runs httpd, sendmail, networking, etc. Then I could have a "user" runlevel that runs xdm, networking, etc.

12.4.2 Init Runlevels

Generally, RH Linux runs in run level 3 – full multiuser mode. The following runlevels are used in RH Linux:

0 Halt.

1 Single user mode.

2 Multiuser mode, without NFS.

3 Full multiuser mode.

6 Reboot.

If your machine gets into a state where it will not boot due to a bad `/etc/inittab`, or will not let you log in because you have a corrupted `/etc/passwd` or have simply forgotten your password, boot into single user mode by typing `linux 1` at the LILO boot prompt. A very bare system will come up and you will be given a shell from which you can fix things.

12.4.3 Shutting Down

To shutdown RH Linux, issue the `shutdown` command. You can read the shutdown man page for complete details, but the two most common usages are:

```
shutdown -h now
shutdown -r now
```

They will each cleanly shutdown the system. After shutting everything down, the first will halt the machine, and the second will reboot.

Avoid running the `reboot` or `halt` commands directly.

12.4.4 In the event of emergency - using rescue.img

There are circumstances that may arise periodically that leave your system in an unstable, even unbootable condition. An improper shutdown caused by a power outage is one such condition. If this should happen to your system the road to recovery begins with three floppy disks. Hopefully you made them during the install (section 6.2) and have them stored in a safe place. If you didn't make them and now need them you should be able to make a set on any PC with a CD-ROM drive. To use your rescue set:

- Boot your boot install floppy
- Insert your ramdisk1 install floppy when prompted

- Insert the rescue floppy when prompted for ramdisk2

This should allow you to restore your system to a functional state.

Chapter 13

Frequently Asked Questions

This section will help you troubleshoot your system. It contains the answers to many common questions, and the solutions to many common problems. Please read it carefully before you ask something on the net. A complete up-to-date version of the Red Hat FAQ is available at:

```
http://www.redhat.com/RedHat-FAQ
ftp://ftp.redhat.com/RedHat-FAQ
```

as well as by fingering or sending mail to *faq@redhat.com*.

13.1 General Questions

13.1.1 Where can I get information on Red Hat Linux?

Contact Red Hat Software for ordering information. The best way is via `http://www.redhat.com`. For other info, send mail to *info@redhat.com* for an automated reply (quite helpful...*really*). You can also poke around `ftp://ftp.redhat.com` and `http://www.redhat.com` for new announcements and product info.

13.1.2 What Media is Red Hat Linux Available on?

It is available on CD and via FTP at this point. To find out where you can FTP it from, see the question on Red Hat Mirrors.

13.1.3 The Red Hat FTP site is *slow*. Are there mirrors?

There are several mirrors of the Red Hat FTP site:

```
ftp.cms.uncwil.edu          /linux/redhat
ftp.wilmington.net          /linux/redhat
ftp.ibp.fr                  /pub/linux/distributions/redhat
ftp.gwdg.de                 /pub/linux/install/redhat
ftp.msu.ru                  /pub/Linux/RedHat
ftp.cvut.cz                 /pub/linux/redhat
sunsite.mff.cuni.cz         /OS/Linux/Distributions/Redhat
ftp.ton.tut.fi              /pub/Linux/RedHat
sunsite.doc.ic.ac.uk        /packages/linux/sun.../dist.../redhat
ftp.funet.fi                /pub/Linux/images/RedHat
gd.tuwien.ac.at             /pub/opsys/linux/redhat
ftp.dstc.edu.au             /pub/linux-redhat
gatekeeper.digital.com.au /pub/redhat
ftp.lab.kdd.co.jp           /OS/Linux/packages/redhat
ftp.pht.com                 /pub/linux/redhat
linux.ucs.indiana.edu       /pub/linux/redhat
ftp.uoknor.edu              /linux/redhat
ftp.cc.gatech.edu           /pub/linux/distributions/redhat
uiarchive.cso.uiuc.edu      /pub/systems/linux/dist.../redhat
ftp.caldera.com             /pub/mirrors/redhat
sunsite.unc.edu             /pub/Linux/distributions/redhat
gatekeeper.dec.com          /pub/linux/redhat
ftp.rge.com                 /pub/systems/linux/redhat
```

The rest of this document has path references to files on these mirrors. Just concatenate that file name to any of the above mirror locations to find the file.

13.1.4 How do I order from Red Hat Software?

```
Red Hat Software Sales can be reached at:
        phone: (203) 454-5500
               (800) 454-5502
        fax:   (203) 454-2582
        email: sales@redhat.com
        WWW:   http://www.redhat.com
```

13.1.5 How do I contact Red Hat Software?

```
Red Hat Software
25 Sylvan Rd South, Suite F
Westport, CT 06880
redhat@redhat.com
(203) 454-5500
(800) 546-7274
(203) 454-2582 (fax)
http://www.redhat.com
ftp://ftp.redhat.com
```

13.1.6 How do I get new updates to Red Hat as they happen?

Keep your eye on:

`current/i386/updates`

on any official mirror for new packages we've made since the current CD-ROM was pressed. Also check the non-free and contrib directories for packages that we can't distribute on CD-ROM or packages that users have sent to us. We will also make periodic announcements to redhat-announce-list mailing list with updates.

13.1.7 How do I get support if I bought the Caldera, PHT, etc CD-ROM?

Purchase of a Red Hat Linux CD-ROM product produced from Red Hat Software entitles you to 30 days of installation support from the Red Hat Support Team. If you purchased Red Hat through another source (Caldera, Pacific Hi-Tech, InfoMagic, Yggdrasil, etc) see `http://www.redhat.com/redhat/support/support.html` for different Red Hat support options.

13.1.8 What is the relationship between Red Hat and Caldera, PHT, etc?

All are separate companies. As with any maker of Linux CD-ROMs, Caldera, Pacific Hi-Tech, Yggdrasil, and LSL are all free to use Red Hat as the basis for their products. This does, however, make those vendors solely responsible for supporting their product if they want it supported. We can not support other vendors products directly, though users of Red Hat from other vendors are welcomed to participate in our mailing lists and make complete use of our WWW site and FTP site. ndexRed Hat Software!mailing lists

13.1.9 What do I do if I have media (manual or CD-ROM) problems?

If you are experiencing problems with the product you received (eg: your manual is missing pages or your CD-ROM is scratched), please contact the Red Hat Software at `sales@redhat.com` or by phone using the above contact information. The problem will be rectified promptly. Please do not report these problems on the `redhat-list` or to `support` as they are likely isolated and your product will simply need to be replaced.

13.1.10 What's the quickest and best way to get support for Red Hat?

You can search for answers to your questions first via `http://www.redhat.com/`.

This has a search engine to search all the Red Hat mailing lists. If you don't find what you need, you can join the redhat-list and then send mail to *redhat-list@redhat.com* with your questions. To subscribe to the list, send mail to *redhat-list-request@redhat.com* with the subject line reading:

subscribe

Due to relatively high traffic on that list, we also have the redhat-announce-list. It is used only for announcements of major concern to the Red Hat community and is low traffic.

To subscribe to the list, send mail to *redhat-announce-list-request@redhat.com* with the subject line reading:

subscribe

We also have a list for developers.

To subscribe to the list, send mail to *redhat-devel-list-request@redhat.com* with the subject line reading:

subscribe

You can also peruse our bug tracking system via the WWW. See `http://www.redhat.com/bugs`. All open and closed bugs are listed there. We are working to improve the speed and layout of the bug tracking system.

13.1.11 How do I report a problem?

Send mail to tech-sup@redhat.com or report the bug to the redhat-list. Again, if you didn't buy Red Hat from us or the ACC Bookstore, please see the previous question, "How do I get support...".

When reporting problems, please be as detailed as possible!!! For example, if you can't get Red Hat to see your SCSI drives, tell us:

- What version of Red Hat
- What kind of SCSI card
- what kernel
- what SCSI id's are the drives

- how many IDE drives do you have
- specific details of the problem

If you can't get your CD-ROM recognized, tell us:

- What version of Red Hat
- make and model of CD-ROM
- type of interface (IDE, SB, etc)
- bootdisk version
- hardware configuration

Again, be as detailed as possible about your problem!

13.1.12 What versions of Red Hat Linux are there?

There have been several. Here's a rundown:

- Preview (or Beta) - Summer '94
- Halloween - Fall '94
- Mother's Day 1.0 - Summer '95
- Mother's Day 1.1 - Late Summer '95
- RedHat 2.0beta - Late Late Summer '95
- RedHat 2.0 - Early Fall '95
- RedHat 2.1 - Late Fall '95
- RedHat Linux/AXP 2.1-Beta - Late Fall '95
- RedHat Linux/AXP 2.1 - January '96
- RedHat Linux 3.0.3 (Picasso) - March '96

13.1.13 What hardware does Red Hat Linux support?

For a current list of supported hardware, please see:

`http://www.redhat.com/`

Look under the Red Hat support section.

13.1.14 How do I get Linux to work with my Adaptec 2940?

Red Hat 2.1 provides several boot images that should work with the 2940. We don't officially support it since there is no 2940 driver in the 1.2.13 kernel distribution, but we are trying to help. None of the images in the `1213` directory support the 2940. You can get images that do support it in the `custom` directory or in the `1332` directory. We suggest using the ones in the `custom` directory. If you can't get those to work, you can try 1.3.32 images. In both cases, please see the next question in the FAQ!

Some tips on getting the drivers to work:

- Disable sync negotiation on the card
- Disable disconnect/reconnect on the card
- Change the transfer rate on *all* devices to 5.0 M/s

All of the above changes need to be made in the 2940 BIOS.

13.1.15 Why won't my Adaptec (274x, 284x) work?

The Adaptec 274x and 284x are supported but may need to be reconfigured to work properly. It has been reported that the wide negotiation on these cards is not quite working, so it should be disabled.

13.1.16 Why don't the 1.3.32 or 2940 images boot in 2.x?

There is a problem with the images in the `1332` and `2940` directory (In versions 2.0 and 2.1). Under DOS, the images are named `filename.img`. In reality, they are really named `filename.img.gz`. These images are compressed using gzip. If you know it, that's fine. All you need to do is copy the image to your hard drive. Then there is the other problem. In the `dosutils` directory there is a copy of `gzip.exe`. It is not the `gzip` program, it is actually a self extracting archive of the gzip program. You need to copy it to your hard drive as well and run it. It will extract itself and some other files.

Once you've gone this far, you can now uncompress your image and write it to floppy. Do the following:

```
move filename.img filename.gz
gzip -d filename.gz
rawrite
```

Then give rawrite `filename` as the file to write to floppy.

Also, you'll notice the IDE/SCSI CD-ROM images don't exist. We removed them due to space requirements. If you require one of them, you should just use the image numbered one higher (the Mitsumi image). It has drivers you don't need, but should still work).

13.1.17 What applications are there for Red Hat Linux?

There are many applications for Linux available. Please see `http://www.redhat.com/` and go to the "Linux Applications and Utilities" section. This section is maintained by a private individual that is not related to Red Hat in any way. You will find information on nearly every product available for Linux on his pages.

13.1.18 Does Red Hat Linux include source code?

Yes. We include the exact source that was used to build the distribution. From release 2.0 on, Red Hat Linux is built on a packaging system called RPM that ONLY uses pristine source (the same as what you'd find at the author's ftp site) and possibly a Red Hat patch. Complete information on RPM is available on `http://www.redhat.com`.

13.1.19 What version of X Windows is included with Red Hat?

Red Hat 2.1 ships two X Windows Servers: XFree86 3.1.2, which is freely distributable and Metro Link X, which is a commercial X server. Both come standard with very nice configuration tools.

13.1.20 Does Red Hat support UMSDOS installs?

In a word, no. It is not a good performance idea. Aside from that, you don't "need" DOS on your machine anyway :-)

13.2 Installation Questions

13.2.1 Do I need swap space?

Yes! If you have 8M of RAM, you *must* enable at least 8M of swap during the installation of Red Hat. If you have more RAM, you should still enable swap, though it isn't mandatory.

13.2.2 I can't get the mouse to work on my Laptop. Why?

Some laptops will report that the "device is in use" when trying to use the mouse. This is most likely due to the fact that the IRQ is getting stolen by the PCMCIA card services package. To fix it, add the following line to /etc/sysconfig/pcmcia:

```
OPTS=irq_mask=0xefff
```

13.2.3 Why doesn't the Linux Library CD work with Red Hat 2.x?

The Linux Library CD-ROM is a.out in nature. You need to install the aout-libs package off your CD-ROM. You can use `glint` or `rpm` to do the install.

It does report that you "do not have a Red Hat system". This is normal. It is really checking for the existence of our old packaging system, RPP. Since we don't use that, it reports that error. You can disregard it and continue the install.

13.2.4 How do I get my IDE CD-ROM on my SB16 to work?

The Creative Labs kit comes with the IDE Interface set to the third IDE port by default (IDE2, I think). This won't work under Linux as it only recognizes two IDE ports. What you need to do is move a jumper on the card to configure it for IDE1 (the secondary IDE port). I'm not sure if you have to make changes under DOS for this configuration to work, but your manuals should help with this (it *will* still work, but you may have to edit a file or two).

You may also have to specify command line parameters like:

```
boot:  linux hdN=cdrom
```

If you have one IDE drive, N is most likely "b" in this case (ie "linux hdb=cdrom"). If you have two, then it will be "c".

13.2.5 How do I get my Sony CDU31 or CDU33 to work?

Under 2.x, the LILO message when you boot the first floppy says:

```
Sony 31&33 CD-ROM REQUIRED        cdu31a=base_addr,[irq|0][,PAS]
```

Under 3.x, this is available on one of the help screens.

"REQUIRED" means just that. There has been a driver change since whatever version you had that requires you to enter a parameter to get the drive recognized. The probe was breaking other things, so they took it out. You need to do something like:

```
LILO boot:  linux cdu31a=0x340
```

If 340 is your base address...and yes, even if you have a 33 use 31a, not 33.

Also, at some point in the install it will ask if you need to enter additional hardware params for LILO. Answer yes, and then enter whatever it was you had to enter above to get the install to work.

13.2.6 Why doesn't my Adaptec 154x work?

It appears that some 1540's and 1542's are a bit hosed by the Buslogic probe. You will usually get an error referring to "DMA" in the Adaptec probe when this happens. To fix it, you need to enter command line parameters as follows:

```
boot:  linux aha154x=0x340 buslogic=0x334
```

This is assuming, of course, that the base address of your Adaptec is 0x340. If not, put your address in there instead. This will force the buslogic to only probe an address where your Adaptec is not.

13.2.7 How do I run the install program again?

Reboot your machine using the three disks that you made for the installation. You will most likely need to completely reinstall your system.

If you just want to reconfigure networking or install more packages, try using the control-panel tools.

13.2.8 Why am I missing some programs?

Try doing a 'df' at the shell prompt. If you have "/" or "/usr" showing up as 100% used, chances are your partition was too small for the entire install. Unfortunately, this does not result in any type of error messages unless you are watching closely (which most people don't when the thing tells you it is going to take 2 hours to install :-). You will most likely need to reinstall and do one of two things: a) make your root or "/usr" partition larger or b) install fewer packages.

Also, if none of the partitions you made for Linux is full, you are probably just missing some packages. You will need to use `glint` or `rpm` to install those.

13.2.9 Do I need to reinstall if I didn't get a LILO prompt?

Not necessarily. You should be able to use the boot disk that you made for the install to boot to your root partition on the hard drive. Insert the disk, reboot the machine, and at the boot prompt, type:

`linux ramdisk=0 root=/dev/xxxx` where xxxx is the hard drive and partition number. If you installed to the first partition of your first IDE drive, this would be hda1. If you installed to the third partition on your second drive, this would be hdb3. The second partition of your second SCSI drive would be sdb2.

If you don't remember, try what you *think* might work. The worst that will happen is a kernel panic or the machine will hang. In either case, reboot and try another partition.

Once you get it booted, you need to edit /etc/lilo.conf and then run 'lilo'. For more info on how to do that properly, you can then read the LILO-HOWTO in "/usr/doc". An example lilo.conf to boot linux and DOS is below:

```
boot=/dev/sda
map=/boot/map
install=/boot/boot.b
prompt
timeout=50
```

```
image=/vmlinuz
                label=linux
                root=/dev/sdb2
                read-only
other=/dev/sda1
                label = dos
```

You may also need a line in the "other" section with "table = /dev/hda" or whatever drive your DOS partition is on. The only lines from above that should change if you boot linux and DOS are "boot", "root", and "other". Some of what is there is optional, like the append and what YOU actually label the dos partition (some people prefer msdos).

One caveat: Make sure the "boot" line points to your first IDE drive, OR your first SCSI drive IF AND ONLY IF you only have NO IDE drives. That is the only way the machine has to know where to find it. You need to also be sure that the partition in the "boot" line is marked "Active" by either the DOS fdisk, or the linux fdisk (or cfdisk). Here are the "rules" of where "/" must live:

1. If you have 2 IDE drives, your root partition MUST live on one of them, NO MATTER WHAT. This also includes any IDE CD-ROM drives on your PRIMARY controller. If you have one IDE hard drive, and one IDE CD-ROM on the PRIMARY controller, you must install your root partition on the IDE hard drive.
2. If you have 1 IDE drive and SCSI drives, your root partition MUST live on the IDE drive or the SCSI drive THAT IS AT ID 0. No other ID's will work.
3. If you have SCSI only, your root partition MUST live on a drive at ID 0 or ID 1. No other ID's will work.

These rules are non negotiable.

BUT I WANT DOS TO BOOT BY DEFAULT!!! Easy. Just change the above /etc/lilo.conf to:

```
boot=/dev/sda
map=/boot/map
install=/boot/boot.b
```

```
prompt
timeout=50

other=/dev/sda1
        label = dos
image=/vmlinuz
        label=linux
        root=/dev/sdb2
        read-only
```

and then run 'lilo' after saving the file.

13.2.10 How do I mount my CD-ROM?

If you installed from CD-ROM, you should be able to do:

`mount /mnt/cdrom`

If you get an error that says the mount point does not exist, do:

`mkdir /mnt/cdrom`

If you did an install via NFS: You need to know what type of CD-ROM you have. The best way is to watch the boot messages as you reboot, or look at /var/adm/messages (`more /var/adm/messages`). You most likely have an IDE CD-ROM that will show up as /dev/hdc or /dev/hdd, or you have a Sound Blaster type that is /dev/sbpcd, or you have a SCSI that is /dev/scd0.

In any case, you can do the following:

`mount -t iso9660 /dev/xxxx /mnt/cdrom`

and substitute xxxx for YOUR device. You can then: `cd /mnt/cdrom` and then: `ls` and you will be looking at the contents of the CD-ROM.

13.2.11 Why does my Trident 9400 show up as an 8900?

XFree86 3.1.2 currently doesn't support the advanced features of the 9400. The timing for the release of the 9400 was just bad for the release dates of 3.1.1, so they weren't able to add the support in. Now that the card is pretty popular and a new release is expected soon of XFree86, we expect to see direct support in the next version of XFree86. For now, you can run resolutions all the way to 1024x768 at 60 hz. If you have trouble using Xconfigurator to set it up, you will probably find that xf86config will do the job (it just doesn't look as nice doing it :-)

13.2.12 Why does Linux only see part of my RAM?

There are a couple things that could be wrong. On *some* 386's, you need to compile your kernel with "Limit memory to 16M?" enabled. Some AMI BIOS motherboards have a memory option to split memory into two segments. I'm not sure what the option is called, but it has something to do with "linear". You'll find it in your BIOS setup. You may need to specify the amount of memory to the kernel at boot time from lilo. To try this, type: `linux mem=32M` at the lilo prompt. If that works, you can add that line to the append in your /etc/lilo.conf and rerun lilo. The example from above would be:

```
append = "mem=32M"
```

Don't forget to run 'lilo' after editing the file.

13.2.13 How do I install to my DOS partition?

You can't. None of the current Red Hat releases support UMSDOS installs. If you have one drive that has one big DOS partition with free space you want to use, you have two options. One is to backup all your DOS data somehow and then repartition the drive into smaller partitions and then restore the DOS data back to a DOS partition. You then have a free partition for linux. The second choice is to use fips. fips is a program that will let you change your partition size of a DOS partition without harming the data on it. It is *STRONGLY* suggested that you backup your data before using fips. Red Hat Software makes no warranties or claims as to the suitability of using fips for this purpose nor can we guarantee that data will remain unharmed. I haven't heard of anyone having a bad experience with fips, but we won't guarantee it, either.

13.2.14 How do I make my own *special* boot disk?

Under 2.x

There are people who have linux installed by some means, but need their own *special* boot disk to install their system. This is possible in some cases. Do not try this with kernels greater than version 1.3.48. It will not work.

First of all, we recommend you only try this with the same kernel source version that we ship (ie 1.2.13 for 2.0 and 2.1). You need to build your kernel on your machine and make sure and say 'y' to the following options during the `make config`:

- CONFIG_MODVERSIONS
- CONFIG_BINFMT_ELF

Then build the kernel with `make dep`, `make clean`, and finally `make zImage`. Once done, your new kernel will be `/usr/src/linux/arch/i386/boot/zImage`. You now need to put it on an install floppy. Under linux, the steps to do this would be something like:

```
dd of=/dev/fd0 if=/path/to/boot/images/boot0000.img
mkdir /mnt/floppy
mount -t ext2 /dev/fd0 /mnt/floppy
cp /usr/src/linux/arch/i386/boot/zImage /mnt/floppy/vmlinuz
lilo -r /mnt/floppy
umount /mnt/floppy
```

You should then be able to reboot with the new floppy and the new kernel.

If you must use a kernel version greater than 1.3.48, you can follow the following steps:

- Make sure and say 'y' to the ramdisk question in `make config`.
- Run “rdev -r <new kernel¿ 49152” on your new kernel.
- Mount the ramdisk 1 floppy image.
- Remove dev/ram2 on the floppy.

- Make a new ram2 with `mknod dev/ram2 b 1 1`
- Unmount the floppy

There will be some weirdness and an error or two displayed as the second ramdisk loads, but it should work.

Under 3.x

You should answer yes to the same parameters as above when building. Then write out a floppy like explained above. Now you can mount it as type "umsdos". Then just copy your new vmlinuz to the root of the floppy and name it "linux" (not "vmlinuz"). It's that easy.

13.2.15 Why can't I get to Unixware now that I've installed Linux?

You need to boot Unixware off of a boot floppy and run 'fdisk /mbr'. That should allow you to get back into Unixware, but will not let you access Linux.

13.2.16 Why won't my Trantor T-130B work?

The Trantor T-130B is really an NCR-5380 in disguise. But, it will most likely not autodetect. You will need to use the NCR boot image along with a boot parameter. The registers are offset by 8 from a normal card. So, for a T-130B at base address 0x350 and IRQ 5, you would use:

```
ncr5380=0x358,5
```

13.2.17 Why does my Diamond do odd things under X Windows?

If you experience problems with XFree86 and your Diamond video card, you may try putting:

```
"Option Diamond"
```

In your /etc/X11/XF86Config (or in /etc/XF86Config if you use that).

13.3 Using Red Hat Linux

13.3.1 Why does Red Hat 'adduser' put each user in his/her own group?

It's called the user group scheme, and it's described in the manual. What it basically does is allow you to use groups to allow multiple people to use a common set of files and edit them, transparently. It goes like this:

- You'd like to have a group of people work on a set of files in say, the "/usr/lib/emacs/site-lisp" directory. You trust a few people to mess around in there, but certainly not everyone.
- So you do "chown -R root.emacs /usr/lib/emacs/site-lisp". And you add the proper users to the group.
- To allow the users to actually create files in the directory you do "chmod 775 /usr/lib/emacs/site-lisp".
- This is fine, but when a user creates a new file it gets the group of the users default group (usually users).
- To prevent this you do 'chmod 2775 /usr/lib/emacs/site-lisp' which causes everything in the directory to get created with the "emacs" group.
- This is fine, but the new file needs to be mode 664 for another user in the emacs group. To do this you make the default umask 002.
- Well, this all works good, except that if your default group is "users", every file you create in your home directory will be writable by everybody in "users" (usually everyone).
- To fix this, you make each user have a "private group" as their default group.

At this point, by making the default umask 002 and giving everyone a private default group, you can easily set up groups which users can take advantage of without doing any magic. Just create the group, add the users, and do the above chown and chmod on the group's directories.

13.3.2 Why doesn't the xmh shipped with Red Hat work properly?

We only ship xmh because it is part of the standard X11 distribution. xmh is basicaly shipped as-is from the X11 distribution, and is most likely broken. We've found that there are several better alternatives. If you want to use mh mail, install the mh RPM and the exmh RPM. exmh is a much better GUI mail reader than xmh.

13.3.3 I rebuilt my kernel, but I got vmlinux instead of vmlinuz. Why?

You need to do `make zImage` or `make zlilo` instead of just `make`. `make zlilo` is the best choice for most beginners as it will not only build the kernel, but also install it as the default for you if the make goes well. Be careful doing this, however, as you will lose your old kernel. `make zImage` will build a compressed kernel and place it in `/usr/src/linux/arch/i386/boot`. You must copy it to your root dir and run lilo yourself to use this one.

If you used make, you got a file called vmlinux. This is an *uncompressed* kernel image, and will NOT work! LILO will only boot a compressed kernel.

13.3.4 I compiled a program, but I can't run it. What gives?

Lets say you do the following as root:

```
gcc -o hello hello.c
hello
```

You'll get "hello: command not found"

Why?

By default, '.' is not in your path. You must run:

```
./hello
```

(dot, slash, h, e, l, l, o with no spaces)

For security reasons '.' should not be in your path.

13.3.5 Why does iBCS break when I recompile my kernel?

You need to answer 'y' to the line that asks:

```
CONFIG_MODVERSIONS [n]
```

If you didn't do that, you'll need to rebuild your kernel and enable it.

13.3.6 Why does Netscape display a ton of errors when I start it?

You didn't read the Netscape installation instructions!

When you untar the distribution of Netscape, you will get an nls directory. Depending on where you untar the distribution, you will need to set some environment variables. You should add lines similar to the following to your `.bash_profile` file:

```
export XKEYSYMDB=${XKEYSYMDB-/home/foobar/lib/X11/XKeysymDB}
export XNLSPATH=${XNLSPATH-/home/foobar/lib/X11/nls}
```

Change the above paths accordingly to reflect the actual location where you installed everything.

13.3.7 Why are include files missing when I try and compile?

You most likely didn't install the kernel sources. Find the sources for the kernel on your system and install them. Then make sure `/usr/src/linux` exists. You may need to make a symlink from `/usr/src/linux` to the directory with your kernel version.

Then you need to `cd /usr/src/linux` and do: `make config` `make` and then you can hit control-C after a few seconds (it makes some symlinks that you might need right at the beginning).

13.3.8 Where is package XYZ?

Before asking where some particular piece of software is (like `diff` for example), please see any RedHat mirror and look in `current/i386/RedHat/rpm-contents.gz`. This file has a query of all available RPMs and their contents. `grep` through it for what you want and it will probably lead you to an RPM that you don't have installed. Use `glint` or `rpm -i` to install the proper RPM.

Also check `current/i386/{updates,contrib,non-free}`.

13.3.9 Why doesn't xtexsh work?

xtexsh is based on older versions of Tcl/Tk than what we ship. Unfortunately, it has not been ported to the newer versions as of yet and it does not work at all.

13.3.10 How do I add nameservers in the netcfg tool?

netcfg is the victim of poor GUI design in the nameserver department. To add a nameserver:

- Click the 'Add' Button
- Click on the '0.0.0.0' entry in the *list* (not in the entry box)
- Edit the '0.0.0.0' in the entry box to your nameservers IP address

- Hit Enter
- That's it!

13.4 Upgrading

13.4.1 I upgraded my kernel to 1.3.x and now PPP doesn't work. Why?

If you upgrade your kernel to a 1.3 kernel, you must use ppp-2.2.0. You can most likely find an RPM for this version on your CD or on ftp.redhat.com.

Appendix A

Licenses

Nearly all of the software components on the Red Hat Linux CD-ROM are freely redistributable. A few of them require special permission to redistribute, and Red Hat Software, Inc. has obtained these permissions. The majority of the software components are distributable under the terms of one of the three licenses in this chapter. Please see each software component for precise distribution terms.

All the software on the CD-ROM produced by Red Hat Software is Copyright (C) 1995 by Red Hat Software, Inc. Unless otherwise noted, all such software is freely redistributable under the terms of the GNU Public License (GPL).

The terms Red Hat, rpm, and glint are trademarks of Red Hat Software, Inc.

A.1 The BSD Copyright

Copyright ©1991, 1992, 1993, 1994 The Regents of the University of California. All rights reserved.

Redistribution and use in source and binary forms, with or without modification, are permitted provided that the following conditions are met:

1. Redistributions of source code must retain the above copyright notice, this list of conditions and the following disclaimer.
2. Redistributions in binary form must reproduce the above copyright notice, this list of conditions and the following disclaimer in the documentation and/or other materials provided with the distribution.
3. All advertising materials mentioning features or use of this software must display the following acknowledgement: This product includes software developed by the University of California, Berkeley and its contributors.
4. Neither the name of the University nor the names of its contributors may be used to endorse or promote products derived from this software without specific prior written permission.

THIS SOFTWARE IS PROVIDED BY THE REGENTS AND CONTRIBUTORS "AS IS" AND ANY EXPRESS OR IMPLIED WARRANTIES, INCLUDING, BUT NOT LIMITED TO, THE IMPLIED WARRANTIES OF MERCHANTABILITY AND FITNESS FOR A PARTICULAR PURPOSE ARE DISCLAIMED. IN NO EVENT SHALL THE REGENTS OR CONTRIBUTORS BE LIABLE FOR ANY DIRECT, INDIRECT, INCIDENTAL, SPECIAL, EXEMPLARY, OR CONSEQUENTIAL DAMAGES (INCLUDING, BUT NOT LIMITED TO, PROCUREMENT OF SUBSTITUTE GOODS OR SERVICES; LOSS OF USE, DATA, OR PROFITS; OR BUSINESS INTERRUPTION) HOWEVER CAUSED AND ON ANY THEORY OF LIABILITY, WHETHER IN CONTRACT, STRICT LIABILITY, OR TORT (INCLUDING NEGLIGENCE OR OTHERWISE) ARISING IN ANY WAY OUT OF THE USE OF THIS SOFTWARE, EVEN IF ADVISED OF THE POSSIBILITY OF SUCH DAMAGE.

A.2 X Copyright

Copyright ©1987 X Consortium

Permission is hereby granted, free of charge, to any person obtaining a copy of this software and associated documentation files (the "Software"), to deal in the Software without restriction, including without limitation the rights to use, copy, modify, merge, publish, distribute, sublicense, and/or sell copies of the Software, and to permit persons to whom the Software is furnished to do so, subject to the following conditions:

The above copyright notice and this permission notice shall be included in all copies or substantial portions of the Software.

THE SOFTWARE IS PROVIDED "AS IS", WITHOUT WARRANTY OF ANY KIND, EXPRESS OR IMPLIED, INCLUDING BUT NOT LIMITED TO THE WARRANTIES OF MERCHANTABILITY, FITNESS FOR A PARTICULAR PURPOSE AND NONINFRINGEMENT. IN NO EVENT SHALL THE X CONSORTIUM BE LIABLE FOR ANY CLAIM, DAMAGES OR OTHER LIABILITY, WHETHER IN AN ACTION OF CONTRACT, TORT OR OTHERWISE, ARISING FROM, OUT OF OR IN CONNECTION WITH THE SOFTWARE OR THE USE OR OTHER DEALINGS IN THE SOFTWARE.

Except as contained in this notice, the name of the X Consortium shall not be used in advertising or otherwise to promote the sale, use or other dealings in this Software without prior written authorization from the X Consortium.

Copyright ©1987 by Digital Equipment Corporation, Maynard, Massachusetts.

All Rights Reserved

Permission to use, copy, modify, and distribute this software and its documentation for any purpose and without fee is hereby granted, provided that the above copyright notice appear in all copies and that both that copyright notice and this permission notice appear in supporting documentation, and that the name of Digital not be used in advertising or publicity pertaining to distribution of the software without specific, written prior permission.

DIGITAL DISCLAIMS ALL WARRANTIES WITH REGARD TO THIS SOFTWARE, INCLUDING ALL IMPLIED WARRANTIES OF MERCHANTABILITY AND FITNESS, IN NO EVENT SHALL DIGITAL BE LIABLE FOR ANY SPECIAL, INDIRECT OR CONSEQUENTIAL DAMAGES OR ANY DAMAGES WHATSOEVER RESULTING FROM LOSS OF USE, DATA OR PROFITS, WHETHER IN AN ACTION OF CONTRACT, NEGLIGENCE OR OTHER TORTIOUS ACTION, ARISING OUT OF OR IN CONNECTION WITH THE USE OR PERFORMANCE OF THIS SOFTWARE.

A.3 Gnu Public License

GNU GENERAL PUBLIC LICENSE Version 2, June 1991

A.3.1 Preamble

The licenses for most software are designed to take away your freedom to share and change it. By contrast, the GNU General Public License is intended to guarantee your freedom to share and change free software–to make sure the software is free for all its users. This General Public License applies to most of the Free Software Foundation's software and to any other program whose authors commit to using it. (Some other Free Software Foundation software is covered by the GNU Library General Public License instead.) You can apply it to your programs, too.

When we speak of free software, we are referring to freedom, not price. Our General Public Licenses are designed to make sure that you have the freedom to distribute copies of free software (and charge for this service if you wish), that you receive source code or can get it if you want it, that you can change the software or use pieces of it in new free programs; and that you know you can do these things.

To protect your rights, we need to make restrictions that forbid anyone to deny you these rights or to ask you to surrender the rights. These restrictions translate to certain responsibilities for you if you distribute copies of the software, or if you modify it.

For example, if you distribute copies of such a program, whether gratis or for a fee, you must give the recipients all the rights that you have. You must make sure that they, too, receive or can get the source code. And you must show them these terms so they know their rights.

We protect your rights with two steps: (1) copyright the software, and (2) offer you this license which gives you legal permission to copy, distribute and/or modify the software.

Also, for each author's protection and ours, we want to make certain that everyone understands that there is no warranty for this free software. If the software is modified by someone else and passed on, we want its recipients to know that what they have is not the original, so that any problems introduced by others will not reflect on the original authors' reputations.

Finally, any free program is threatened constantly by software patents. We wish to avoid the danger that redistributors of a free program will individually obtain patent licenses, in effect making the program proprietary. To prevent this, we have made it clear that any patent must be licensed for everyone's free use or not licensed at all.

The precise terms and conditions for copying, distribution and modification follow.

A.3.2 GNU GENERAL PUBLIC LICENSE

TERMS AND CONDITIONS FOR COPYING, DISTRIBUTION AND MODIFICATION

0

This License applies to any program or other work which contains a notice placed by the copyright holder saying it may be distributed under the terms of this General Public License. The "Program", below, refers to any such program or work, and a "work based on the Program" means either the Program or any derivative work under copyright law: that is to say, a work containing the Program or a portion of it, either verbatim or with modifications and/or translated into another language. (Hereinafter, translation is included without limitation in the term "modification".) Each licensee is addressed as "you".

Activities other than copying, distribution and modification are not covered by this License; they are outside its scope. The act of running the Program is not restricted, and the output from the Program is covered only if its contents constitute a work based on the Program (independent of having been made by running the Program). Whether that is true depends on what the Program does.

1

You may copy and distribute verbatim copies of the Program's source code as you receive it, in any medium, provided that you conspicuously and appropriately publish on each copy an appropriate copyright notice and disclaimer of warranty; keep intact all the notices that refer to this License and to the absence of any warranty; and give any other recipients of the Program a copy of this License along with the Program.

You may charge a fee for the physical act of transferring a copy, and you may at your option offer warranty protection in exchange for a fee.

2

You may modify your copy or copies of the Program or any portion of it, thus forming a work based on the Program, and copy and distribute such modifications or work under the terms of Section 1 above, provided that you also meet all of these conditions:

a. You must cause the modified files to carry prominent notices stating that you changed the files and the date of any change.

b. You must cause any work that you distribute or publish, that in whole or in part contains or is derived from the Program or any part thereof, to be licensed as a whole at no charge to all third parties under the terms of this License.

c. If the modified program normally reads commands interactively when run, you must cause it, when started running for such interactive use in the most ordinary way, to print or display an announcement including an appropriate copyright notice and a notice that there is no warranty (or else, saying that you provide a warranty) and that users may redistribute the program under these conditions, and telling the user how to view a copy of this License. (Exception: if the Program itself is interactive but does not normally print such an announcement, your work based on the Program is not required to print an announcement.)

These requirements apply to the modified work as a whole. If identifiable sections of that work are not derived from the Program, and can be reasonably considered independent and separate works in themselves, then this

License, and its terms, do not apply to those sections when you distribute them as separate works. But when you distribute the same sections as part of a whole which is a work based on the Program, the distribution of the whole must be on the terms of this License, whose permissions for other licensees extend to the entire whole, and thus to each and every part regardless of who wrote it.

Thus, it is not the intent of this section to claim rights or contest your rights to work written entirely by you; rather, the intent is to exercise the right to control the distribution of derivative or collective works based on the Program.

In addition, mere aggregation of another work not based on the Program with the Program (or with a work based on the Program) on a volume of a storage or distribution medium does not bring the other work under the scope of this License.

3

You may copy and distribute the Program (or a work based on it, under Section 2) in object code or executable form under the terms of Sections 1 and 2 above provided that you also do one of the following:

a. Accompany it with the complete corresponding machine readable source code, which must be distributed under the terms of Sections 1 and 2 above on a medium customarily used for software interchange; or,

b. Accompany it with a written offer, valid for at least three years, to give any third party, for a charge no more than your cost of physically performing source distribution, a complete machine-readable copy of the corresponding source code, to be distributed under the terms of Sections 1 and 2 above on a medium customarily used for software interchange; or,

c. Accompany it with the information you received as to the offer to distribute corresponding source code. (This alternative is allowed only for noncommercial distribution and only if you received the program in object code or executable form with such an offer, in accord with Subsection b above.)

The source code for a work means the preferred form of the work for making modifications to it. For an executable work, complete source code means all the source code for all modules it contains, plus any associated interface definition files, plus the scripts used to control compilation and installation of the executable. However, as a special exception, the source code distributed need not include anything that is normally distributed (in either source or binary form) with the major components (compiler, kernel, and so on) of the operating system on which the executable runs, unless that component itself accompanies the executable.

If distribution of executable or object code is made by offering access to copy from a designated place, then offering equivalent access to copy the source code from the same place counts as distribution of the source code, even though third parties are not compelled to copy the source along with the object code.

4

You may not copy, modify, sublicense, or distribute the Program except as expressly provided under this License. Any attempt otherwise to copy, modify, sublicense or distribute the Program is void, and will automatically terminate your rights under this License. However, parties who have received copies, or rights, from you under this License will not have their licenses terminated so long as such parties remain in full compliance.

5

You are not required to accept this License, since you have not signed it. However, nothing else grants you permission to modify or distribute the Program or its derivative works. These actions are prohibited by law if you do not accept this License. Therefore, by modifying or distributing the Program (or any work based on the Program), you indicate your acceptance of this License to do so, and all its terms and conditions for copying, distributing or modifying the Program or works based on it.

6

Each time you redistribute the Program (or any work based on the Program), the recipient automatically receives a license from the original licensor to copy, distribute or modify the Program subject to these terms and conditions. You may not impose any further restrictions on the recipients' exercise of the rights granted herein. You are not responsible for enforcing compliance by third parties to this License.

7

If, as a consequence of a court judgment or allegation of patent infringement or for any other reason (not limited to patent issues), conditions are imposed on you (whether by court order, agreement or otherwise) that contradict the conditions of this License, they do not excuse you from the conditions of this License. If you cannot distribute so as to satisfy simultaneously your obligations under this License and any other pertinent obligations, then as a consequence you may not distribute the Program at all. For example, if a patent license would not permit royalty-free redistribution of the Program by all those who receive copies directly or indirectly through you, then the only way you could satisfy both it and this License would be to refrain entirely from distribution of the Program.

If any portion of this section is held invalid or unenforceable under any particular circumstance, the balance of the section is intended to apply and the section as a whole is intended to apply in other circumstances.

It is not the purpose of this section to induce you to infringe any patents or other property right claims or to contest validity of any such claims; this section has the sole purpose of protecting the integrity of the free software distribution system, which is implemented by public license practices. Many people have made generous contributions to the wide range of software distributed through that system in reliance on consistent application of that system; it is up to the author/donor to decide if he or she is willing to distribute software through any other system and a licensee cannot impose that choice.

This section is intended to make thoroughly clear what is believed to be a consequence of the rest of this License.

8

If the distribution and/or use of the Program is restricted in certain countries either by patents or by copyrighted interfaces, the original copyright holder who places the Program under this License may add an explicit geographical distribution limitation excluding those countries, so that distribution is permitted only in or among countries not thus excluded. In such case, this License incorporates the limitation as if written in the body of this License.

9

The Free Software Foundation may publish revised and/or new versions of the General Public License from time to time. Such new versions will be similar in spirit to the present version, but may differ in detail to address new problems or concerns.

Each version is given a distinguishing version number. If the Program specifies a version number of this License which applies to it and "any later version", you have the option of following the terms and conditions either of that version or of any later version published by the Free Software Foundation. If the Program does not specify a version number of this License, you may choose any version ever published by the Free Software Foundation.

10

If you wish to incorporate parts of the Program into other free programs whose distribution conditions are different, write to the author to ask for permission. For software which is copyrighted by the Free Software Foundation, write to the Free Software Foundation; we sometimes make exceptions for this. Our decision will be guided by the two goals of preserving the free status of all derivatives of our free software and of promoting the sharing and reuse of software generally.

11

NO WARRANTY

BECAUSE THE PROGRAM IS LICENSED FREE OF CHARGE, THERE IS NO WARRANTY FOR THE PROGRAM, TO THE EXTENT PERMITTED BY APPLICABLE LAW. EXCEPT WHEN OTHERWISE STATED IN WRITING THE COPYRIGHT HOLDERS AND/OR OTHER PARTIES PROVIDE THE PROGRAM "AS IS" WITHOUT WARRANTY OF ANY KIND, EITHER EXPRESSED OR IMPLIED, INCLUDING, BUT NOT LIMITED TO, THE IMPLIED WARRANTIES OF MERCHANTABILITY AND FITNESS FOR A PARTICULAR PURPOSE. THE ENTIRE RISK AS TO THE QUALITY AND PERFORMANCE OF THE PROGRAM IS WITH YOU. SHOULD THE PROGRAM PROVE DEFECTIVE, YOU ASSUME THE COST OF ALL NECESSARY SERVICING, REPAIR OR CORRECTION.

IN NO EVENT UNLESS REQUIRED BY APPLICABLE LAW OR AGREED TO IN WRITING WILL ANY COPYRIGHT HOLDER, OR ANY OTHER PARTY WHO MAY MODIFY AND/OR REDISTRIBUTE THE PROGRAM AS PERMITTED ABOVE, BE LIABLE TO YOU FOR DAMAGES, INCLUDING ANY GENERAL, SPECIAL, INCIDENTAL OR CONSEQUENTIAL DAMAGES ARISING OUT OF THE USE OR INABILITY TO USE THE PROGRAM (INCLUDING BUT NOT LIMITED TO LOSS OF DATA OR DATA BEING RENDERED INACCURATE OR LOSSES SUSTAINED BY YOU OR THIRD PARTIES OR A FAILURE OF THE PROGRAM TO OPERATE WITH ANY OTHER PROGRAMS), EVEN IF SUCH HOLDER OR OTHER PARTY HAS BEEN ADVISED OF THE POSSIBILITY OF SUCH DAMAGES.

END OF TERMS AND CONDITIONS

A.3.3 Appendix

How to Apply These Terms to Your New Programs

If you develop a new program, and you want it to be of the greatest possible use to the public, the best way to achieve this is to make it free software which everyone can redistribute and change under these terms.

To do so, attach the following notices to the program. It is safest to attach them to the start of each source file to most effectively convey the exclusion of warranty; and each file should have at least the "copyright" line and a pointer to where the full notice is found.

```
<one line to give the program's name and a brief idea of
what it does.> Copyright (C) 19yy <name of author>

This program is free software; you can redistribute it
and/or modify it under the terms of the GNU General Public
License as published by the Free Software Foundation;
either version 2 of the License, or (at your option) any
later version.

This program is distributed in the hope that it will be
useful, but WITHOUT ANY WARRANTY; without even the implied
warranty of MERCHANTABILITY or FITNESS FOR A PARTICULAR
PURPOSE. See the GNU General Public License for more
details.

You should have received a copy of the GNU General Public
License along with this program; if not, write to the Free
Software Foundation, Inc., 675 Mass Ave, Cambridge, MA
02139, USA.
```

Also add information on how to contact you by electronic and paper mail.

If the program is interactive, make it output a short notice like this when it starts in an interactive mode:

```
Gnomovision version 69, Copyright ©19yy name of author
Gnomovision comes with ABSOLUTELY NO WARRANTY; for details
type 'show w'.  This is free software, and you are welcome
to redistribute it under certain conditions; type 'show c'
for details.
```

The hypothetical commands 'show w' and 'show c' should show the appropriate parts of the General Public License. Of course, the commands you use may be called something other than 'show w' and 'show c'; they could even be mouse-clicks or menu items–whatever suits your program.

You should also get your employer (if you work as a programmer) or your school, if any, to sign a "copyright disclaimer" for the program, if necessary. Here is a sample; alter the names:

```
Yoyodyne, Inc., hereby disclaims all copyright interest in
the program 'Gnomovision' (which makes passes at
compilers) written by James Hacker.
```

```
<signature of Ty Coon>, 1 April 1989 Ty Coon, President
of Vice
```

This General Public License does not permit incorporating your program into proprietary programs. If your program is a subroutine library, you may consider it more useful to permit linking proprietary applications with the library. If this is what you want to do, use the GNU Library General Public License instead of this License.

Index

V

W

X

Y